PEACE THEOLOGY
AND VIOLENCE AGAINST WOMEN

ELIZABETH G. YODER, EDITOR

OCCASIONAL PAPERS NO. 16

Institute of Mennonite Studies
3003 Benham Avenue
Elkhart, Indiana 46517

1992

Occasional Papers

Occasional Papers is a publication of the Institute of Mennonite Studies and authorized by the Council of Mennonite Seminaries. The four sponsoring seminaries are Eastern Mennonite Seminary (Harrisonburg, VA), Goshen Biblical Seminary and Mennonite Biblical Seminary (Elkhart, IN), and the Mennonite Brethren Biblical Seminary (Fresno, CA). The Institute of Mennonite Studies is the research agency of the Associated Mennonite Biblical Seminaries.

Occasional Papers is released several times yearly without any prescribed calendar schedule. The purpose of the *Papers* is to make various types of essays available to foster dialogue in biblical, theological and practical ministry areas and to invite critical counsel from within the Mennonite theological community. While most essays will be in finished form, some may also be in a more germinal stage--released especially for purposes of testing and receiving critical feedback. In accepting papers for publication, priority will be given to authors from the CMS institutions, the college Bible faculties in the Council of Mennonite Colleges, the associate membership of the Institute of Mennonite Studies, and students and degree alumni of the four seminaries.

Because of limited circulation of the *Occasional Papers,* authors are free to use their material in other scholarly settings, either for oral presentation at scholarly meetings or for publication in journals with broader circulation and more official publication policies.

Orders for *Occasional Papers* should be sent to the Institute of Mennonite Studies, 3003 Benham Avenue, Elkhart, IN 46517-1999.

ISBN 0-936273-20-8
Printed in the USA

TABLE OF CONTENTS

CONTRIBUTORS

Gayle Gerber Koontz, Ph.D. is Dean at Associated Mennonite Biblical Seminaries.

Mary H. Schertz, Ph.D. (candidate), is Assistant Professor of New Testament at Associated Mennonite Biblical Seminaries.

Lydia Neufeld Harder is a doctral candidate at Toronto School of Theology.

Lois J. Edmund, Ph.D., is a psychologist and student of theology in Winnipeg, Manitoba.

Isaac I. Block, Ph.D., is Assistant Professor of Contemporary Ministries at the Mennonite Brethren Bible College in Winnipeg, Manitoba.

Carolyn Holderread Heggen, Ph.D., is Professor of Counseling at Webster University and Therapist/Supervisor at Family Therapy of Albuquerque.

Ruth E. Krall, Ph.D. is Associate Professor of Religion and Psychology and Director of Peace Studies at Goshen College.

Miriam E. Martin, Ph.D., R.N., is Professor and Director of the Department of Nursing at Goshen College.

Carol Penner is a doctoral student in theology at the Toronto School of Theology.

Harriet Sider Bicksler is Director of the Board for Brotherhood Concerns of the Brethren in Christ Church.

PREFACE

On October 4 and 5, 1991, a bold experiment took place at Associated Mennonite Biblical Seminaries. Theologians and therapists met together to consult with one another about the subject of violence against women. Sponsored by the AMBS Women's Advisory Committee in cooperation with the Institute of Mennonite Studies and the Peace Studies program, the primary purpose was, "to assemble persons from Peace Church traditions who have dealt with the topic of violence against women and/or peace theology in a scholarly or professional way to identify issues, to shape the future directions of peace church reflection and practice in relation to violence against women, and to encourage further work on the issues."

How would it work to have the theologians present papers and the practitioners respond to their work? The approximately 120 participants and listeners assembled with a great deal of anticipation. The process, which had been in the planning stages for over a year, involved the traditional reading of papers and formal responses, but added discussion groups in which the invited practitioners--pastors, counselors and therapists--interacted with theologians to bring their experience with victims, and in some cases their own victimization, to bear on their theological work.

A secondary purpose was to invite preparation of material that might be published afterwards to stimulate broader conversation among Mennonites and peace church dialogue on this issue. Those invited to present papers represented different disciplines--biblical studies (Mary Schertz), theology and ethics, (Gayle Gerber Koontz and Carol Penner), pastoral theology (Isaac Block), and pastoral psychology (Ruth Krall). The papers proved to be stimulating and eminently publishable. This volume is the result.

A third purpose was to strengthen the community of peace church Christians working in the these two areas (violence against women and peace theology) for mutual support, inspiration and learning. The consultation, though not without its stresses and strains, certainly clarified the issues and extended the boundaries of the discussion, as this collection will show.

The consultation and this collection of papers would not have been possible without the hard work of the planning committee: Ann Keener Gingrich, Martha Smith Good, Karla Kauffman, Gayle Gerber Koontz, Elizabeth Yoder, and especially the careful and tireless attention of Lynell Bergen, who served as chair. Ross T. Bender of the Institute of Mennonite Studies who administered the project was an invaluable resource as was Ted Koontz of the Peace Studies Program and his assistant, Jean Hirschler. Wilma Cender spent many hours assisting Ross in bringing the consultation to reality and also prepared the manuscript of this book for publication.

This volume is offered with the hope that it will contribute to the overall purpose of promoting shalom between women and men.

Elizabeth Gingerich Yoder
February 26, 1992

INTRODUCTION

Gayle Gerber Koontz

Mennonites have only recently begun to recognize violence against women as an issue for reflection in relation to Mennonite "peace theology." To my knowledge, one of the first papers on this topic at a formal, more than local gathering of theologians/ethicists was Vange Willms Thiessen's "Case Study on Domestic Violence: A Theology of Peace and a Theology of Liberation," presented at the Peace Theology Colloquium in Vancouver in June 1991. To be sure, Mennonite psychologists and pastors have been researching and raising issues related to family violence and violence against women, and peace educators have emphasized the importance of peacemaking beginning with the family. But most scholarly Mennonite work in the theology and ethics of pacifism has focused its attention historically, and continues to focus currently on specific issues other than domestic violence and violence against women.

Why aren't we paying attention to this reality in theological and ethical reflection? Ordinary *lethal* violence against women is more frequent than violent incidents in Ireland, yet it is not clearly engaged in our peace agenda. Unfortunately it may be partly because of its very ordinariness. Studies have shown that in one in four marriages there is some violence. Isaac Block's work in this volume shows us that Mennonites are no exception. We also need to remember that it is only with the most recent wave of feminism beginning in the early 1970's that basic information about violence to and violation of women became widely available and noticed in North America. Silence and sexism have blinded us from attending to this issue.

But also significant, I believe, is the fact that historically most Mennonite peace theology and ethics has been engaged with questions of and arguments for Christian pacifism in the face of violence that was being justified by others. Catholic, Lutheran, and Calvinist traditions developed complex systems of theological-ethical thought justifying violence in war. Some Christians have argued on behalf of capital punishment, and so forth. There is no comparable major Christian tradition which has sought to explicitly justify the use of violence against women. On the surface, such violence has been assumed to be wrong (therefore ethical debate was not needed) while actual practice has frequently been cloaked in silence and self-deception.

While there are theological beliefs or interpretations that enable this self-deception or excuse violence, and there have been periods when persecution of witches (primarily women), for example, was justified with theological argument, there is no current debate among Christian ethicists regarding the justification of violence against women as there continues to be regarding violence in war and revolutionary situations. The response to the recent Gulf War is an example.

Since there is no major ethical debate among Mennonites or Christians about the acceptability of violence against women, what is the task of those entering and participating in peace theology conversations with reference to this concern? It seems to me that we have been invited to pool our resources toward the following ends:

1. *Increase the scope of peace theology agenda.*

By attending to violence toward and violation of women, we open the "private" spheres of the household and of sexuality, two overlooked and fundamental areas of life, for reflective formulation and testing of a Christian ethic of peace. Ethicist Karen Lebacqz[1] points out that Christians need to do work in this area because typical approaches to sexual ethics are not adequate since "they presume an equality, intimacy, and safety that does not exist for women" (p.4). Lebacquz goes so far as to suggest that for many women the very attempt to form a heterosexual relationship in some cultural contexts, including contemporary America, can be seen as an exercise in "loving your enemy" (p. 4).

2. *Urge the agenda.*

The task here is to identify for the church that violence against women is a unique and important reality for peace theology because of the way it focuses issues of men's power and women's power in relation to God's power and purposes on earth. We need to see the links between theology, gender, power and violation. In a startling example of this linkage, Chaim F. Shatan[2] cites a young airman who flew in Vietnam for seven years, but who resigned from the Naval air arm on the first day he actually saw what he was shooting at. "I saw three men run out of the underbrush," he said. "At first I shot to kick up some dust at their heels and make them run faster; then I aimed carefully and fired again. One man fell; one man blew up; and to my horror, I noticed I had a hard on!...That night I went to the flight surgeon who tried to convince me that there was nothing to worry about--my experience was very common; I'd get used to it" (p. 40).

We have not paid enough attention to how sexuality and

violence, eroticism and male dominance have been linked in
socialization and experience. Dominance has been eroticized; both
women and men find male power and female powerlessness sexy.
This is undergirded by general patterns of social interaction in which
men are expected to be dominant and women are expected to be
submissive, according to Lebacqz (p. 7). Mennonites have not significantly challenged this cultural pattern.

3. *Help pose issues and provide analysis.*

Here our task is to identify aspects of theological and ethical
definition and debate that impact thinking and response to violence
against women. One task is to assist with sorting out the language
we use in our moral discourse. For example, what behaviors do we
include when we talk about "violence" to women? How do we define
violence?

Or again, what difference does a woman's "consent" make in
whether an action is right or wrong? How is consent to be defined?
When is submission "consent"? The following letter to "Dear Abby"
illustrates this dilemma:

> Dear Abby: A friend of mine was picked up and
> arrested for raping a 24-year-old woman he had
> dated twice. He had sex with her the first time he took her
> out. He said she was easy. The second time she gave him
> the high-and-mighty act and refused to have sex with him.
> Now he's got a rape charge against him, which I don't think
> is fair. It seems to me if she was willing to have sex with
> him on the first date, there is no way she could be raped by
> him after that. Am I right or wrong?[3]

"'Normal' patterns of male-female sexual relating in this culture are defined by patterns of male dominance over women," writes
Marie Fortune.[4] "Hence our earliest socialization teaches us to con-
fuse sexual activity with sexual violence" (p. 22). So how do we
define rape?

Or further, of particular interest to peace church people, what
is the meaning of nonresistant love or love of enemies in relation to
violence against women. My paper in this volume attempts to work
with some of these questions.

4. *Evaluate theological and ethical convictions and cultural assump-*
tions with reference to violence to/violation of women.

This task involves identifying and eschewing theological interpretations or ethical categories which, along with socio-cultural

4   Peace Theology and Violence

assumptions, enable self-deception or excuse violence against women. Isaac Block, Carol Penner, and Ruth Krall each assist us with this task in various ways in this volume. Not all suffering is meaningful and witnesses to the quality of God's love and power; obedience to parents is not an unambiguous virtue. Nonresistance defined as passivity betrays and traps women who are the ones most vulnerable to violence and violation.

5. *Offer constructive proposals.*

We have the opportunity to reframe or propose theological interpretations and ethical procedures or principles which can undergird an ethic of peace and justice for and between Christian women and men. This is the task to which Mary Schertz and I, in particular, set ourselves in this collection.

6. *Call for integration and consistency of theology and practice.*

This task calls for us to join with others to unmask self-deception in terms of what is going on among Christians so that our practice can become consistent with our purposed ethical commitments. Theological and ethical reflection is carried on in order to better understand how our Christian convictions and commitments (along with many other factors) relate to practice--how they indirectly contribute to violation of women and/or how they enable women and men to respectfully love each other. Given the realities of our lives, reflective examination of practice in relation to violence to/violation of women is essential in maintaining the integrity of a Mennonite peace theology conversation and witness.

Finally, reflective examination of this issue in relation to peace theology by the church may help prepare us to better minister to and share God's good news in Christ to neighbors caught in cycles and webs of gender-linked violence.

NOTES

1. "Love Your Enemy: Sex, Power and Christian Ethics," in *The Annual of the Society of Christian Ethics 1990*, ed. D.M. Yeager. (Distributed by Georgetown University Press, Washington, D.C.).
2. "The Entrails of Power: Bogus Manhood and the Language of Grief," *Women and Men: The Consequences of Power.* ed. Dana Hiller and Robin Ann Sheets. (Cincinnati, Ohio: Office of Women's Studies, University of Cincinnati, 1977).
3. Cited in Lebacqz, p. 4, from the *San Francisco Chronicle*, January 7, 1990.
4. *Sexual Violence: The Unmentionable Sin* (New York: Pilgrim Press, 1983), p. 22.

Chapter 1

CREATING JUSTICE IN THE SPACE AROUND US: TOWARD A BIBLICAL THEOLOGY OF PEACE BETWEEN WOMEN AND MEN

Mary H. Schertz

In an article in the *Journal of Marital and Family Therapy,* Vicky Whipple says that "domestic violence occurs in families of all religious backgrounds. . .A battered woman who has deep religious convictions needs assistance not only with ending the abuse she has been experiencing, but also with addressing the religious issues that are involved."[1] It is a sad fact that violence is a reality in some Mennonite homes and that our theological convictions have sometimes contributed to this on-going problem in ways in which until recently we have been largely unaware. Part of the foundational impetus for the gathering here today is the painful insight that the convictions about peace that we hold most dear and that are profoundly resonant with our very peoplehood have sometimes proved to be "bad news" for those who struggle with violence in the home.[2]

As Mennonites, our convictions about not resisting evil and about accepting suffering as a positive value[3] have contributed to a tolerance of some reprehensible actions. On the more positive side, our common concern for issues of peace has prepared us to think about violence against women as a justice issue. We are fortunate to have an exegetical and theological base upon which we can begin to construct a biblical theology of peace between men and women. Such a base will help to ground our actions and guide our struggle to deal decisively with the violence in our homes.[4]

My intention for this presentation is fourfold. First, I will place before you some of the assumptions I bring to the task. Second, I will make a case for the importance of a biblical theology of peace between men and women. Third, I want to assess the current status of the intersection of biblical peace theology with the concern for violence against women. Fourth, the greater part of our time together will be spent looking at some specific themes that are important to a shalom biblical theology and asking what kinds of expansion, modification or alterations are suggested by the specific concerns of violence against women. Our aim will be to consider the broad parameters of a biblical theology of peace between men and women and to make some proposals for future studies.

ASSUMPTIONS

In accordance with good feminist practice, let me begin by outlining some of the assumptions which lie behind my attempt to think about biblical theology from the perspective of how it can help us speak to the issues of violence against women.[5] One of my basic assumptions is simply that relations between men and women in North American Mennonite homes are too often characterized by violence.[6] Sometimes this violence is perpetrated by women upon men, but more often it is inflicted by men upon women. Whether the level of violence among us approaches and perhaps surpasses the level of violence in families of the general society is in some ways immaterial. *Any* level of violence among Christians responsible for transmitting a peace tradition is too high.

A second assumption is that this violence, though often hidden from view, affects us all. The trauma of the family sitting in the pew in front of us touches us and diminishes us whether we know about the violence or not. While there is not time to argue this claim, it can be supported both from the view of traditional Christian theology, which understands the body of Christ as an organic unity, and from the view of feminist theology, which understands all forms of life to be interconnected.[7]

A third assumption is that as pastors, we have contributed to a toleration for this family violence by valuing the permanence of marriage above the sanctity of personhood. The logic of protecting the illusion of a marriage covenant already broken by violence escapes me. Such thinking, it seems to me, erodes irrevocably the ideal of marriage itself. I will say more about this point later. A corollary assumption is that as members of the body of Christ we have contributed to the violence by accepting silence as a way of dealing with it. There are many needs in the church and many issues claiming our attention. It is not my expectation that everyone here will make family violence their "issue." But whether it is our issue or not, each of us has a God-given responsibility not to cover up something horrible with silence. Knowledge entails responsibility, and not to speak jeopardizes our very humanity.

A final assumption is personal. I approach these issues as one who continues to love both the church and the Bible--sometimes against my better judgment and sometimes in the face of the very real appeal offered by indifference. As Beverly Harrison has suggested in an article she titled "The Power of Anger in the Work of Love," the opposite of love is not anger or, I would add, even hate; but rather apathy or indifference.[8] It is true that the collusion of the church in the domination of women and the use of the Bible against the victims of violence, whether advertent or inadvertent, makes me angry. It is, however, an anger born of caring. You may find yourself agreeing or disagreeing with my positions. But to hear me accurately you will need to hear me as one who stands within the problems and possibilities of the church--inseparably a lover and a protester.

WHY A *BIBLICAL* THEOLOGY OF PEACE BETWEEN WOMEN AND MEN

It seems to me that the situation in which we find ourselves as a church community--a state of professing peace while harboring violence--is intolerable. This situation demands that we take another look at the bedrock theological convictions that support our common life. We need a biblical theology of peace between women and men. This theology must support our saying a resounding "no" to violence against women. It must support a clear and consequential understanding that the sanctity of marriage depends upon upholding the sanctity of the persons within marriages. It must support the difficult and morally demanding movement from silence and passivity to speech and action.

While the most important reason to revise and reformulate our thinking is the pastoral concern of healthy relationships, the larger issues of the mission of the church and the peace witness of the Mennonite expression of faith are also at stake. That mission and witness are founded upon our identity as a peace church. If we cannot live justly and non-violently in our own homes, how can we take a peace stance in the world? Where is our credibility? Where is our integrity? Stopping the horrible things that are happening in our families, creating justice in the space around us, offering the safety that is the will of a loving and providential God to every member of the church family is simply imperative for the integrity of who we are and the credibility of what we represent.

What we do here today and tomorrow also has ramifications for the wider church community as well as our denomination. We have much to offer, perhaps especially in the areas of our peace concerns. But I think we have sometimes entered into these conversations with some naiveté and some arrogance. Taking a serious internal look at how we have failed to live peacefully among ourselves, in our most intimate and loving circles, will chasten us. What we will then have to offer the wider debates will of necessity be a more soberly considered peace position, a position disciplined and tested by an honest reflection upon the experience of the violence suffered by women in their Mennonite homes as well as other experiences

with the problems of the world in which we live.
In order to begin speaking internally and externally about
these issues we will need to do some new work. Part of the work
which needs to be done is in the area of biblical theology. First and
foremost, we are a biblical people. Decry as we must the growing
biblical illiteracy in the churches, bemoan as we will the growing
influence of theologies that are not as closely connected with Scripture as some of us would like, the Bible still constitutes the common
ground of our discourse. It is where we meet. Disagreeing as we do
on doctrines of inspiration and issues of methodology, arguing as we
do over what the word of God means for our day, we can and will
continue to find our collective spirituality in the pages of the text.
Because it is both our common and contested ground, any serious
attempt to deal with the issues of violence theologically must give
some serious attention to biblical theology.

TAKING STOCK

When we talk about the intersection between a biblical theology of peace and the issues of violence against women we are in
something of new territory on three counts. First, as Perry B. Yoder
notes, while we have studied peace fairly intensively from a variety of
points of view, the Mennonite theological leadership has not "spoken
clearly about the centrality of peace to the biblical message."[9]
Although the picture has improved in the last eight years,[10] we are
nevertheless not abounding in thorough-going and comprehensive
efforts at doing shalom biblical theology. You will note later that I
make a rather deliberate effort to connect my suggestions toward a
biblical theology of shalom between men and women with some of
the more general work that has been done on a shalom biblical
theology.[11]
Second, while much work has been done addressing such
issues as war, the role of the state, economics and international relations, interaction between people, the substance of relationship, has
rarely if ever been considered as an issue of justice worthy of analysis from a peace theology perspective.[12] Even Mennonite work with
mediation and reconciliation issues has emphasized listening and
negotiating skills rather than systematic analysis of the power and
institutionalized inequities operative in interpersonal relationships.
Therefore a biblical theology of peace and justice between men and
women brings a new question to the discussion.
Third, while a good deal of feminist work has been done in
the areas of exegesis, hermeneutics and theology, not much has been
done in the area of feminist *biblical* theology. In fact, in a 1989 arti-

cle in which she makes a tentative proposal for a feminist biblical theology, Phyllis Trible contends that though the time has come to begin making some overtures between feminist hermeneutics and biblical theology, the "season" has not yet come to write it. That task, in her opinion, awaits further exegetical work.[13]

The lack of foundational work in some of the areas crucial to the task of formulating a biblical theology of shalom between men and women may be a reason to proceed with some caution. It is, nevertheless, not a reason to abandon the project. Whatever we accomplish will be necessarily tentative and open to review and revision. In that respect, a biblical theology of peace between men and women shares the situation of both biblical shalom theology and feminist biblical theology. All are beginning enterprises sharing the excitement and the pitfalls of most new ventures. Therefore, granting the necessary cautions, let us also indulge our hopes in the exuberance of new possibilities, new work to be done, new frontiers to explore. Formulating a biblical theology that speaks to a specific area of shalom concerns can be a stimulating challenge.

WHAT WOULD A BIBLICAL THEOLOGY OF PEACE BETWEEN MEN AND WOMEN LOOK LIKE?

There is no real consensus among scholars as to what biblical theology is, nor any definitive notion of how one goes about doing it. Trible states rather engagingly that "biblical theologians, though coming from a circumscribed community, have never agreed on the definition, method, organization, subject matter, point of view, or purpose of their enterprise."[14] Given that theoretical quagmire, my solution is to ignore it and simply get on with the task. For the sake of grounding the enterprise as much as seems feasible, however, I suggest we consider Ben C. Ollenburger's definition of the purpose of biblical theology--especially as it seems particularly apt in light of the questions before us. Ollenburger suggests that biblical theology is responsible for "guarding, enabling and critiquing the church's self-conscious reflection on its praxis."[15] By this standard, the criterion of highest importance for a biblical theology of peace between men and women is its potential for helping the church reflect upon how believers interact with one another as women and men.

Furthermore, in order to connect these suggestions with ongoing work in shalom biblical theology, I suggest that we take as our methodological starting point for this enterprise Yoder's notion that any biblical theology which purports to make sense of the biblical materials needs to integrate six "cardinal points" or biblical themes.

These themes are: creation, covenant, community, cult, cross, and consummation. In "Toward a Shalom Biblical Theology" Yoder sketches briefly how the concept of shalom integrates these themes.[16] I would like to look at each of them with a view to the questions and insights raised by a focus on peace between men and women. The expectation is not that a biblical theology of peace between men and women will emerge from this exercise, but that these considerations might point toward and perhaps guide the kind of work that needs to be done to arrive at such a theology.

CREATION

There is no single story which has had a greater impact on the lives of modern women, both secular and religious, than the biblical creation accounts--and much of that influence has been negative. Much of the historic denigration of women, including their domination by husbands, has been justified by citing an interpretation of these stories that assumes the subjection of women as part of the divine order. Fortunately, in this instance, a good deal of solid exegetical work has been done that challenges the repressive interpretation and offers alternative explanations. These alternative interpretations vary considerably in methodology and emphasis. At the heart of most of them, however, lies the observation that the subordination of the first woman is the result of sin and not an expression of the Creator's intention.[17]

If we have available to us some interpretations of the creation accounts that respect the texts and are liberating for women, can we incorporate those into a peace theology that speaks to the issues of violence against women? While a full exploration of this question clearly lies beyond the scope of this paper, let me sketch some parameters and make some suggestions for further study.

Yoder suggests that a shalom biblical theology understands that the creation is good and that the Creator God is active in the on-going transformation of both matter and history. Our experience of the lack of shalom, in this case the situation of violence between men and women with all its causes and all its consequences, is the result of human rejection of the divine perspective. The future, however, is not closed but open to transformation. Therefore, the human task is to use the opportunity that lies between the limitations of our human perspective and our trust in a God who transforms matter and history to create shalom.[18]

A task of prime importance for a shalom biblical theology between men and women, then, is two-fold. The first part of the job is to describe the difference between the divine and human perspectives on human gender. We must try to recapture the mind and heart of God with respect to our creation as women and men: the blessedness of being created female, an image of the divine; the blessedness of being created male, an image of the divine. Part or perhaps most of this work, I suggest, will need to be done by women for themselves and men for themselves. Some of it will likely need to be done by women and men together.

The second part of the job is to suggest actions to be taken that are expressions of trust in a God who transforms relationships between men and women. Part of this work will need to be critical and part of it constructive. Gaining clarity about our own blessedness as sexual beings may help us acquire the keen perception we need to discern how we have institutionalized the opposite of that blessedness in our social structures. Gaining such clarity may also instill in us the security we need to tear down what needs to be torn down and to build what needs to be built.

These critical and constructive tasks of a shalom biblical theology between men and women will not be easy. It will involve hard work with the texts that speak to the mind and heart of God on the issues of shalom and gender. It will mean dealing honestly and rigorously with the difficulty of the New Testament misinterpretations of the Genesis material.[19] It will also mean unlearning our socialization and being both confrontive and humble with each other while we struggle to more accurately reflect the mind of God on our creation as male and female. Difficult as this process may be, however, there may be no more significant task of biblical theology.

COVENANT

The theme of covenant has not been used against women to the extent that the creation theme has been. Yet, of the two, covenant may prove to be the more difficult theme for a theology of biblical shalom between men and women. The reason for the difficulty is the connection between the concept of covenant and the sovereignty of God. More precisely, while God's sovereignty itself may not be so problematic, the theology of submission that sometimes follows from that doctrine has been problematic for some battered women.

Again, we will begin our exploration by summarizing a peace theology view of covenant and then outlining some of the major problems and possibilities from the perspective of a theology of shalom between men and women. Yoder suggests that the purpose of covenant is "to restore God's sovereignty and shalom among human kind." God's act of grace to Israel was an act of justice and liberation. Israel responded by recognizing the sovereignty of God and declared allegiance by obeying the Torah. Living in accordance with the covenant law, then, is the heart of the establishment of a community of justice and peace, a community of shalom.[20] While covenant, grace and justice are important concepts for a biblical theology of peace between women and men, the conjunction of shalom and sovereignty raises something of a dilemma for many of the persons who would benefit most from such a theology. On the one hand, the metaphors of sovereignty--God as King, Jesus as Lord, and related terms--are, I would argue, intrinsic to any biblical theology. (While the use of the term "sovereign" softens the concept and renders it more inclusive, it does not mitigate the preponderance of the usage nor its centrality in the biblical materials.) On the other hand, disempowered people, who have literally experienced being ruled, legitimately raise the question of whether there is anything that can be understood as God-like in the concept of sovereignty.

In response to this question, I suggest, there are two issues worthy of reflection and study. The first is the question of what kinds of meanings and possibilities might be derived from a consideration of God's sovereignty as iconoclastic. In *Sexism and God-Talk*, Rosemary Radford Ruether talks about the "liberating sovereign." To claim a divine sovereign frees one from all human sovereigns. As Ruether admits, however, this theological move is much clearer when the symbolism is used by groups of believers who are marginalized in their societies. For those believers who are part of the dominant class the distinction between God's sovereignty and that of human lordships is much more difficult to maintain.[21] Still, exploration of this possibility would be profitable for the formulation of our project.

The other issue worthy of reflection and study has to do with personal autonomy in relation to God's sovereignty. While the issue has taken different forms in different historical and cultural settings, I would argue that in our context the crux of the matter is experiential and has more to do with the issues of personal autonomy than domination as such. Without getting deeply into the debates about the differences between men and women and the causes of those differences, we can perhaps posit that behind the debate about the usefulness or uselessness of theological images and metaphors of God's sovereignty lie different experiences of personal autonomy. Most men take personal autonomy for granted; many if not most women do not. While this difference may be more perceptual than actual,[22] it stands to reason that the act of conversion, the act of turning from sin and aligning oneself with the purposes of God finds different expressions in light of different experiences of personal autonomy. For someone to whom personal autonomy is a given, the alignment may well take the form of surrender of the pseudo-independent self to the larger, transcendent and truer Self of God. This concept of salvation speaks to the sins of the powerful. The sovereignty of God has one cluster of meanings in that setting. For someone to whom personal autonomy is not a given, joining the movement of God in history may well mean assuming greater personal autonomy as one perceives and accepts the responsibility for a call or mission that is uniquely one's own. This concept of salvation speaks to the sins of the disempowered. Sovereignty takes on other clusters of meaning in that setting.

What is needed from the perspective of a biblical theology of shalom between men and women is a closer look at the question of submission and personal autonomy in light of the biblical understandings of the sovereignty of God. On the one hand, those of us who have denounced the metaphors of sovereignty may need to question the automatic correlation of the images of God as King and Jesus as Lord with our suspicions of, and rejections of domination. Before we assume that these images are negative for oppressed peoples, we ought to look at what they mean in their biblical contexts. Do not these images essentially call for alignment with the projects of God, for loyalty to and the keeping of faith with these projects? Are not these associations meanings which we can affirm? On the other hand, those of us who have clung nearly literally to the metaphors of sovereignty may need to question the correlation between the use of these metaphors and the structures of dominance which maintain oppression. From the standpoint of a biblical theology of shalom between men and women it is imperative that we formulate a theology of God's sovereignty that is not oppressive so that women and men may with equal joy enter into a covenant with God and with each other that enables the establishment of communities of justice and peace.

COMMUNITY

It is to those communities of justice and peace that we now turn. As we have already noted, a shalom theology perspective views the establishment of the shalom community as the result of God's acts of grace and justice. Shalom is actualized within the community when the community keeps the covenant.[23]

From the standpoint of a biblical theology of peace between men and women, there is little with which to take issue in this basic formulation. However, there is a problem with the way in which contemporary concepts of community have been integrated with notions of sin, sacrifice and the role of the individual within the community. In this case, contemplation of the issues of peace between men and women can perhaps provide a corrective.

In our effort to disassociate ourselves from the abuses of western individualism, we have introduced ideas and practices that come very close to sacrificing the sanctity of the individual for the good of the community into our theological understandings. Isaac Block, from whom we will be hearing more later, reports that Winnipeg Mennonite pastors are ambivalent about whether they are as committed to the sanctity of personhood as they are to the permanence of marriage--as evidenced by the fact that over 80% of the pastors surveyed would advise endangered women to stay in the home while seeking counseling.[24]

From the point of view of a shalom biblical theology more generally as well as a specific theology of peace between men and women, this kind of thinking represents a significant theological error. In an article entitled "The Biblical Grounding of Human Value," Moshe Greenburg contrasts the Hebrew understanding of human nature with the understandings of other Ancient Near Eastern civilizations. A study of the laws concerning human life reveals that Israel broke decisively from the utilitarian or instrumental view of human value that prevailed in the surrounding cultures. In these other cultures one could compensate for a murder with goods and possessions, or sometimes slaves and children. In Israel, however, murder was punishable by death. Whereas the Hebrew death sentence might appear to be the more primitive, Greenburg argues that the penalty actually evidences a higher valuing of human life than that of the surrounding cultures. In other words, the Hebraic law is founded upon an understanding that the value of the human person is beyond the reach of other values. Human life can not be measured by or compensated for with values of property, money or the equivalences of other persons. Paradoxically to be sure, but nevertheless really, the intent of the Hebrew death penalty for murder was to render the taking of life unthinkable, an act against the Creator of human life and personality that could not be mitigated by human recompense.[25]

What began in the Hebrew Bible with a decisive move away from a view of the human as a tool, a means to an end, developed in both the Mishnah (and, I would argue, the New Testament) into an awareness of the "infinite worth of individuality." The Mishnah expresses awe and gratitude that each human is created unique and unlike any other human in time and space.[26] In the New Testament teachings and parables of Jesus there is the same concern for human value and regard for the individual. In the parable of the Good Shepherd, for instance, the value of the individual is placed equal to or perhaps higher than the value of the community. Or perhaps more accurately, the peril of the individual within the community is also the peril of the community. The ninety-nine sheep are left to wander in the wilderness until the one is restored to them. The lost coin, the lost son, the saying that the Sabbath is made for humanity, not humanity for the Sabbath and numerous other teachings can also be read in light of the sanctity of personhood.

A biblical theology of shalom between men and women calls for a new and closer look at the values of the individual and the community. To speak thus is in no way to advocate western individualism, with its pervasive competitive ethos and pleasure principle. To speak thus is to advocate an assignation of values in line with the biblical valuing of persons *and* communities--both values are irreducible. Communities should not be exploited for the aggrandizement of the individual. Nor should individuals be sacrificed for the community. Communities which violate the sanctity of the people in them are not communities in the biblical sense. Marriages which violate the sanctity of the persons in them are not, I would suggest, marriages in the biblical sense. Recognizing the value of individuals and recognizing that this value is the bedrock of community and the institutions of community is not a way of taking community or marriage less seriously. Rather, it is a way of taking them more seriously--holding them to the highest kind of idealism.

CULT

A shalom biblical theology regards cult, or the public practice and maintenance of community, as consisting of "common worship, confession, forgiveness, and restitution." It restores shalom between members of the community when it is broken and it places the people of the community into the presence of God where they may experience the mystery of the God who sustains them.[27]

Again, this formulation serves as a good foundation for a biblical theology of peace between men and women. In addition to these concepts, the specifics of peace-making between men and women call us to three additional considerations. The intersection of a peace theology of worship and the issues of violence against women summon us: 1) to another look at what constitutes true purity or morality within the worshipping community; 2) to another look at the worshipping community as the body of Christ and what it means when the bodies of part of that body are violated; 3) to

another look at the issue of trust between members of the worshipping community.

First, a biblical theology of peace between men and women
summons us to examine prevailing concepts of purity in our experience of common worship. In his book on the economic emphases in
the gospel of Luke, Halvor Moxnes argues that Jesus' criticism of
the establishment religious leaders and their concern for purity is
rooted in his understanding of true purity and false purity. The leaders were attending to the minute points of purity and missing the
point of having a pure heart before God--which requires the doing of
justice.[28]

Just as Jesus called the religious establishment of his day to a
new assessment of morality, so the issues of violence against women
call us to reevaluate what is truly pure and what is truly an abomina-
tion. A biblical theology of peace between men and women which
purports to take into account the experience of violated women calls
for a reassessment of morality. There are some very difficult questions which need to be answered in light of the silence which has
protected the perpetrators of family violence among us. There are
questions about *what kinds of sins* come to the light of examination
by the community. There are questions of *whose sins* come to the
community's attention. There are questions about how *the issue of
gender* figures into our assessments of what is acceptable and what is
not acceptable, what is pure and what is impure among us. These
are not easy questions. They may be divisive. They will certainly tax
our emotions and our intellects in ways that we can only imagine.
But the questions and the conversations they elicit are vital to peace-
making between men and women. They are vital to the health of
our practice of community and our worship of God.

The second consideration evoked by a theology of peace
between men and women follows from the first. Both the writer of
the gospel of John and the apostle Paul connect the concept of the
temple, as the center of the people's experience with God, with the
body of Christ. In John 2:13-22, the temple is connected with the
person of Jesus; in Paul, with the body of believers gathered in the
name of Christ.[29] In our formulation of a theology of peace between
men and women we might find it profitable to consider whether the
violation of women's bodies and spirits does not constitute a violation of the temple, the body of Christ. Just as human bloodshed in
the temple defiled the sanctuary of God and made it unfit for the
meeting of divine and human in worship, so the violation of persons
within our worshipping bodies renders us unable or less able to
come close to God, to be known by and to know God. Just as the
defilement of the temple redounded to the entire community as well

as the guilty person, so the one who violates other persons diminishes the relationship between the whole church and God.

In this connection, we might also be reminded that the only recorded instance of Jesus using physical force is the temple cleansing in John's gospel. Without getting into the pacifist debates that have swirled about this passage, let us simply note that the violation of the temple evoked a most serious response from Jesus, even, some might say, an extreme response. Perhaps the situation of violated women, a situation that I suggest violates us all at the very heart of our relationship to God, demands our anger, our very serious response, our extreme action.

A final issue raised by the concept of cult has to do with trust. Worship is an act that requires trust. It requires letting go the self to contemplate and enjoy the Self of God. The believer must be able to trust God. It also requires letting go the self to join with others in that contemplation and enjoyment. When a person's trust is broken by those whom they love, the loss to the individual and to the body of Christ is in some senses irrevocable. There is no more serious matter before the worshipping community than the fact that we have been silent in the face of trust destroyed. How can we worship? Who shall ascend the hill of the Lord? And who shall stand in the holy place? Those who have clean hands and pure hearts.[30]

CROSS

A shalom biblical theology defines the cross as a major symbol of "the power of God in making shalom through the defeat of evil." Since the cross is the act that defines God most fully, according to this view, it becomes a model for the shalom-making acts of the community of God's people. The way of suffering love, which has as its purpose the reconciliation of humankind to God, is the way to make peace.[31]

This focus on the symbol of the cross, which has been central to Mennonite doctrine and practice for the entire history of our peoplehood, can be discomforting when viewed from the perspective of violence against women. Our theology of suffering love has in reality contributed to and even increased the endangerment of the victims of family violence among us. The ethos of suffering love practiced by the wives of abusive husbands has produced not shalom but its opposite.

Certainly the practice of suffering love has never been based on efficacy. We have concentrated on being faithful, rather than being successful--content to leave the matter of results in the hands of God. The trouble is that not only is suffering love not effective in

situations of family violence, but in some cases it is a contributing
factor in escalating the cycle of violence. We are faced, I think, with
a serious challenge to one of our most profoundly held and treas-
ured theological convictions.[32]

As a way of beginning the discussion that must necessarily
and with urgency take place among us on this issue, I offer two
tentative theses from the perspective of biblical theology. The first is
an affirmation of the cross in an ultimate sense. Ultimately, the project of God is a project accomplished through suffering or nonviolent
love. In the last resort, when the choice really was a choice between
returning, reversing or perpetrating violence on the one hand and
absorbing violence into his own body on the other hand, Jesus made
a clear choice--and died on the cross. Violence simply could not
and cannot accomplish God's ultimate goal of transforming enemies
into friends. The atonement was accomplished on the cross because
ultimate reconciliation depended upon ultimate loyalty to the methods and means of God. A biblical theology of peace between men
and women, if it is to be a *biblical* theology that is, must necessarily
honor the text in this regard.

The second tentative thesis from the perspective of biblical
theology is rooted in the observation that the cross was not the first
resort but the last resort. I suggest that our theology of the cross
lacks clarity about means and ends as well as timing. The
crucifixion did not take place before its time. The event of the cross
took place only when the options were limited to either absorbing
violence or returning it in kind. In other words, Jesus did not seek
the path that led to his death. He sought, rather, to announce the
good news to the poor and to call for a renewal in the way people
thought about morality and justice as well as in the way they related
to one another. Making these choices did indeed lead to his
crucifixion. But before that crucial moment, there were first
speeches and sermons, private interviews, public denunciations,
demonstrations, examples, stories, healings, exorcisms, the calling of
an alternative community, and so forth. In short, the cross was a
means, not an end in itself, and it was a means of last resort. It was
the course chosen only when the alternative was abandonment of the
project, only when the choice really was between absorbing the
violence or perpetrating it through acquiescence or retaliation.

Taking these considerations into account raises the question
of whether taking up one's cross, which is a daily necessity according
to the gospel, means not so much setting one's course by the star of
suffering love as setting a course which involves announcing good
news to the oppressed and living a new relationality. Running this
course demands all the confrontation, healing, strategizing, persua-

sion, denunciation, parables and demonstrations of which we are capable. And, yes, as a last resort it demands the cross--but not as an end in itself and not as a first resort, or even an intermediate resort. To accept and to absorb violence prematurely is neither true to the biblical portrayal of the cross nor an effective resource against violence--since such action leads only to more violence. Such a view of the cross, it seems to me, may open up new possibilities for genuine service, repentance, prophecy and creative confrontation with the powers of violence on a variety of levels while, at the same time, criticizing the false service of perpetrating violence through acquiescence.

CONSUMMATION

A shalom biblical theology view of consummation or the end of history is fundamentally a trust that the historical process has a point to it that makes sense. History is a partnership between God and the people of God. The people of God respond to the graceful acts of God, acts of liberation and transformation, by making peace. It is not ours to determine the end of history but to trust the God in whose hands that end resides.[33]

Feminist theologians and feminist interpreters of Scripture have not invested a great deal of energy in the issues of eschatology as a theme for constructive theological work. The theme of hope has largely been cast in terms of transformation and reform within the church and the society rather than in a concept of the end of history. I want to raise the question of whether those of us who work toward formulating a theology of peace between men and women can afford to ignore the questions of eschatology. While I would agree that particulars detailing the end of history may not be of great interest, a hope that makes sense of history is of vital importance to a biblical theology of shalom between men and women.

Perhaps this conversation about hope and history needs to begin with the observation that the personal journey of a peace activist[34] has stages of denial, anger and despair--and a kind of hope that corresponds to each stage. When one is engaged in the pre-critical stage, the stage of denial, the kinds of hope offered by traditional theology suffice. When one is engaged in the critical stage, the stage of anger, the revolutionary hope of liberation theology will suffice. I suspect that there is, however, a third stage. Whereas the transition between the first and second stages always and necessarily involves moving into action, the third stage may not entail any sort of change in the activist's behavior. The activist remains active but begins to move into an awareness of the true size of the problem.

This awareness radically alters one's perspective on one's own effectiveness. In that sense, this third stage is a post-critical stage. It is a time in which the peace activist comes to understand that despite protest, despite activism of the most profound sort, one will nevertheless continue to live one's life and die one's death in the context of that which one is protesting and against which one is acting. Not only do we live within the contexts of patriarchalism, racism, militarism and economic exploitation, but we live diminished lives within these contexts. The structures of oppression are wasteful of human potential--sapping the peoples' energy, resources and creativity as well as the capacity for love. Perceiving the wasteland usually involves confronting despair. It is not a passive response, because one arrives at this level of knowledge only through commitment to and continued practice of activism. Most poignantly, the question becomes a question of how we go on living and laughing after we acknowledge that the forces diminishing us will continue to diminish us and our children and our children's children. The question becomes one of how we wrest meaning from this absurdity. What is responsibility and what is hope in the face of the persistence of these evils despite our continued best efforts?[35]

It is for precisely this expression of chastened and honed commitment that a vigorous and imaginative theology of the sense and purpose of history needs to be very carefully developed as a component of a biblical theology of shalom between men and women. At some point, one must choose between absurdity and hope in a God to whom and in whom history makes sense, a hope that transcends our lifetimes and is larger than ourselves. A biblical theology of peace between men and women must also be a theology of hope.

CONCLUSIONS

What I have tried to do here is to sketch some broad parameters for the kind of work that needs to be done, the kind of issues that need to be raised and the kind of questions that should be asked as we move toward a biblical theology of shalom between men and women. There would be other ways of arranging and ordering such a theology, but I have found it useful to think in terms of creation, covenant, community, cult, cross and consummation under the larger rubric of a shalom biblical theology. My hope is that a clearer understanding of God's mind about us as men and women will enable us, as men and women together to say a resounding and uncompromising NO to the violence that is eating away at the heart of our peoplehood. But more than that, my hope is that a clearer understanding of God's delight in us as men and women may help us delight in ourselves and each other. May we know full well the joy of shalom.

NOTES

1. Vicky Whipple, "Counseling Battered Women from Fundamentalist Churches," *Journal of Marital and Family Therapy*, Vol. 13, No.3 (1987), 251.

2. In his book *Revolution from the Heart*, Columban priest Niall O'Brien speaks of the painful moment when he realized that the church's response to the situations of violence in the Philippines "was inadequate and at times added to the problem." He describes the way in which the Columban community school for the poorer people was "twisted" to serve the purposes of the Marcos regime (Oxford University Press, 1987, 74). The position of the Mennonite church in relation to violence against women may be somewhat analogous to this. It is deeply disturbing to realize that the good we try to do with our peace theology may in certain situations have been distorted and twisted to serve the purposes of evil.

3. The point that traditional Mennonite nonresistance is not resistant toward evil and accepts suffering as a Christian virtue is debatable. Much depends upon how one reads Guy F. Hershberber's classic *War, Peace, and Nonresistance* (Herald Press, 1944). It is true that Hershberger keeps before his reader the premise that God is a God of justice and wrath, the final arbiter of rewards and punishments (17ff). Nonresistance is, in that sense, not refusing to oppose evil but deferring to the One who properly resists evil. It is also true that to assume, for instance, that Hershberger's discussion of the superiority of love over justice (49, 216-217) can or does speak to issues of systemic violence within communities of faith is anachronistic at best. Nevertheless, even though Hershberger's positions may be more nuanced than commonly portrayed and even though he obviously was not thinking about the issue of violence against women when he wrote, the fact remains that some of these themes have been misused in the church's response to the violence in some Mennonite homes.

4. At the consultation at which this paper was presented, my use of male scholarship was offensive to some people. Since any attempt to build upon the exegetical and theological base our tradition of peace theology has provided necessarily entails the use of male scholarship, I accept the ambivalence of such usage along with its potential. The questions raised by using concepts and constructs formulated by men for feminist inquiry are important ones.

My position in this paper has its basis in two premises. First, I value the work that has been done in the historic peace church tradition as a foundation for working at the theological components of the issue of violence against women. This work, which has largely been done by men, must indeed be used critically and reflectively. In my opinion, however, it remains an entry point that has integrity for women of the peace church tradition. Furthermore, part of the value that Mennonite women's voices have for the larger enterprise of feminist thought and life depends upon our careful use of the tradition we represent. The second point is simpler. Truth is not gender specific and truth is of paramount importance. While it is vital to take seriously questions of context, such as the gender and power of the speaker, it is also vital not to ignore questions of content and truth.

5. One of the basic tenets of feminist thought and practice is the exposure of all scholarship as imbued with bias rather than neutral or objective. (See Fiorenza, *In Memory of Her*, xx-xxiv, for one discussion of this idea.) In keeping with this understanding, many feminist thinkers begin their analysis with a report of their assumptions.

6. While I am not excluding considerations of other forms of violence against women such as rape, I am mainly concerned with family violence. The reason for this focus is a judgment that it is this aspect of the issue that most urgently requires a biblical foundation for changing the way we see each other and act toward each other as men and women. We do not need the Bible to teach us that rape is wrong. We do need the Bible to teach us that the terrorization and subjugation of women in their homes does not reflect the mind of God.

7. For a basic discussion from the perspective of traditional Christian theologies I find Hendrikus Berkhof's discussion of the nature of the church as the body of Christ very helpful. (*Christian Faith: An Introduction to the Study of the Faith*, trans. by Sierd Woudstra, Eerdmans, 1979, 392ff.) For a basic feminist perspective see chapter 9, "The New Earth: Socioeconomic Redemption from Sexism," of Rosemary Radford Ruether's *Sexism and God-Talk: Toward a Feminist Theology*, (Beacon Press, 1983, 214-234). The last part, 232-234, is especially illustrative of this point.

8. Beverly Wildung Harrison, "The Power of Anger in the Work of Love: Christian Ethics for Women and Other Strangers," *Union Seminary Quarterly Review* 36 (1981), 41-57.

9. Perry B. Yoder, "Toward A Shalom Biblical Theology," *Conrad Grebel Review*, 1,3 (fall, 1983), 39.

10. Most markedly with the publication of Yoder's *Shalom: the Bible's Word for Salvation, Justice, and Peace* (Faith and Life, 1987) but also note the forthcoming Institute of Mennonite Studies six volume series on shalom biblical theology to be published by John Knox/Westminster.

11. The semantic fields of the Hebrew word "shalom" and the English word "peace" do not exactly correspond. See Yoder, *Shalom*, 10-23. In this essay, however, I am using them interchangeably and somewhat critically. By both shalom and peace, I mean profound well-being encompassing all the realms of human life— social, physical, spiritual, political, economic, etc. In this usage, neither term should be understood to mean quietude or harmony without justice.

12. Yoder's *Shalom* book lays the foundation for such an analysis from a biblical theology point of view, but he does not take this crucial step. This omission constitutes the most substantive criticism I would have to offer his very helpful and

ground-breaking treatment of the subject.

13. Trible, "Five Loaves and Two Fishes: Feminist Hermeneutics and Biblical Theology," *Theological Studies* 40, 1989, 289.

14. *Ibid.*, 282.

15. Ben C. Ollenburger, "Biblical Theology: Situating the Discipline," in *Understanding the Word: Essays in Honor of B.W. Anderson* edited by Butler, Conrad and Ollenburger, JSOT, 1985, 53.

16. Yoder, "Toward. . .," 45. There would be other outlines, other thematic suggestions that could also be used to construct a biblical theology of peace between men and women. In fact, in his book *Shalom*, Yoder works more intensively with such themes as justice, law, salvation, atonement, the state, etc. The greater detail of *Shalom* is helpful and would lend itself to a profitable examination from the perspective of a biblical theology of peace between men and women. At this beginning point, however, the broader scope of the six themes cited in the article is, in my judgment, more useful to the overview task.

17. The literature is substantial. In addition to numerous articles, three major treatments demonstrating some of the different approaches are: Phyllis Trible, *God and The Rhetoric of Sexuality,* Fortress, 1978, 72-165; Carol L. Meyers, *Discovering Eve: Ancient Israelite Women in Context,* Oxford, 1988; Mary Hayter, *The New Eve in Christ: The Use and Abuse of the Bible in the Debate about Women in the Church,* SPCK/Eerdmans, 1987.

18. Yoder, "Toward. . .," 45.

19. See Hayter, *New Eve* (131-133), for an excellent discussion of the use of the Genesis material in 2 Corinthians 11:13 and 1 Timothy 2:11-15.

20. Yoder, "Toward. . .," 45.

21. Ruether, 64.

22. That is to say that the issue as I perceive it is not a question of whether men or women have more personal autonomy. That seems a useless generalization. My point is that many women can not assume that they will obtain or maintain personal autonomy without working for it. Autonomy for women is usually won and protected through struggle. For men, it is assumed.

23. Yoder, 45.

24. Isaac I. Block, "Mennonite Pastors' Response to Domestic Abuse," *Journal of Mennonite Studies* 8 (1990), 193,196.

25. Moshe Greenburg, "The Biblical Grounding of Human Value," in *The Samuel Friedland Lectures 1960-1966,* New York: Jewish Theological Seminary of America, 1966, 45.

26. *Ibid.*, 47-50.

27. Yoder, 45.

28. Halvor Moxnes, *The Economy of the Kingdom: Social Conflict and Economic Relations in Luke's Gospel,* Fortress, 1988, 99-126.

29. See Barbara Bowe's "'You are the Body of Christ': Paul's Understanding of the Human Person," *The Bible Today* (May, 1991), 139-144 for an overview of the Pauline concept of the body as a "unique description of the church" (139).

30. Paraphrase from Psalm 24.

31. Yoder, "Toward...," 45.

32. Clearly, it can be argued that contemporary expositions of suffering love are far more nuanced than this brief summary indicates and that a more carefully nuanced view of the cross does not lend itself to the kind of misuse to which I am pointing here. See relevant sections of C. Norman Kraus' *Jesus Christ our Lord: Christology from a Disciple's Perspective* (Herald Press, 1987) and Harry Huebner's "Christology: Discipleship and Ethics" in *Jesus Christ and the Mission of the Church: Contemporary Anabaptist Perspectives*, edited by Erland Waltner (Faith and Life, 1990), 56-73 for two different approaches to a contemporary enunciation of a theology of the cross. While I am grateful for these and other efforts, it is also clear that at the congregational level a simpler and more basic understanding of the cross has contributed to women's pain. The question is whether this problem can be solved with more sophisticated exposition or whether the fundamentals of the doctrine need to be examined. I do not know the answer. It is a serious question and one to which the issues of violence against women call us to attend.

33. Yoder, 45.

34. Among whom I would number anyone working correctively and redemptively in the area of the relationships between men and women as well as anyone working on the task of constructing a biblical theology of peace between men and women.

35. Some of the questions raised here emerged in another written context. See Mary H. Schertz, "Response to the Responders," in *Perspectives on Feminist Hermeneutics*, edited by Gayle Gerber Koontz and Willard Swartley, Institute of Mennonite Studies, 1987, 127.

RESPONSE

Lydia Neufeld Harder

It is always easier to dialogue with those person with whom one shares basic assumptions and commitments. I am happy to respond to this paper because I too stand in that ambiguous place where love for the church and the Bible is intertwined with anger and pain at the way the Bible and theology have contributed to the violence against women. I too am committed to breaking the silence in theological and church circles, a silence which permits us as a Mennonite church to espouse a peace theology while harboring violence in our midst. I too struggle to name the "bad news" in our peace theology while attempting to proclaim the "good news" which God has for us.

Mary's paper begins by exploring the reasons why we must give serious attention to biblical theology as part of the way of dealing with the issue of violence. This is not self-evident to feminists who insist that theological reflection must begin with experience. I would like to expand on Mary's discussion by using a metaphor which can help us reflect on our complex and contradictory relationship to the Bible. I would like to reflect on what it means to confess that the Bible is our "home," a home that has at times been dysfunctional, but one which can help us regain a sense of truly being "at home."[1]

There are a number of ways in which we can think of the Bible as our home. It is in the Bible where the stories are told of our origins and where we as Christians were first named. In the Bible those decisive events which formed our identity as family of God are told and retold. Many of the crucial arguments between us were already begun and carried on within the biblical forum. Our most intimate feelings have been expressed within this sphere. We can rebel and leave our home, but it will always be there as we struggle to find a sense of identity in our own time and context.

As with any home, it will be very difficult for us to come to terms with our heritage if we cannot admit its humanness. One way to look at this human factor is to begin to examine the voices which interact within the biblical conversation. Though there are many voices which speak, some voices are loud and dominant; others are almost silenced, hidden and marginalized. The stories of the kings, of male prophets are told more eloquently and with more detail than the stories of mid-wives, of home-makers and of slaves. The male-centeredness (androcentrism) of the Bible needs to be acknowledged so that we can ask a deeper question. Which voices speak the truth, identifying that which is of God and that which holds the members of the Christian family together? Which of the many interpretations of our family experiences express the essence of home for us?

Perhaps our family discussions will become more sensitive and open if we begin to listen to the marginal voices in our home. Perhaps healing will come as we open ourselves to the stories of pain and anger even within the Bible. As every member of the family begins to share in the interpretation of the past we will come to terms with some family secrets which were hidden in the closet. But it is only in taking this risk that marginal persons and even strangers will begin to feel "at home" in our midst.

This shift in the way we listen to the biblical conversation will mean a similar shift in our theological methodology. We will need to become self-conscious about the reasons in our own *experience* which lead us to emphasize certain biblical passages to the exclusion of others. It is this connection of biblical theology to experience which opens a space for a new look at Mennonite peace theology and violence against women. Biblical theology will change if interpreters with different experiences begin to read and interpret the Bible.

A recognition that interpreter and text form two poles of the dialogical interpretive process means that we must become aware of how our biases influence our biblical theology. The choices of our conversation partners become an ethical issue. We need to become more conscious of how power relationships influence the theological conversations in which authoritative interpretations of the Bible arise.

Mary's paper struggles to set new directions in biblical theology by speaking from the viewpoint of someone who stands in solidarity with women affected by male violence. In her discussion of the themes of peace theology she points out a number of crucial areas that need more work. I want to speak to several of the areas that she refers to and add a few additional comments.

1. *Our creation theology will be greatly affected if we begin with the experience of disharmony and violence between women and men.* We will then be listening most closely to those voices within the Bible which speak of healing and of hope. We will not primarily be concerned to describe an ideal state of shalom. Rather we will identify various situations of disharmony in the pages of the Bible and note how God's creative power worked to create new relationships of love and respect between people. The focus will be on

recognizing and accepting the gift of God's healing work among us. Part of that gift will include a new understanding of ourselves and the other in the image of a creating healing God, thus challenging us and empowering us to become co-creators in this healing process.

2. *Our covenant theology will need to come to terms with the kinds of power relationships which our theological language has idealized.* The metaphors of sovereignty for God have included images of power which we experience as dominating and controlling. The metaphors of our human position have emphasized images of subjection and impotence. Thus covenant relationships, whether between God and humanity or between women and men are often understood as oppressive rather than freeing and empowering, especially when God and men are identified as the powerful and dominant partner.

What is needed is another look at the human temptation to see God in our own image, a temptation which was already there in the patriarchal setting of the biblical world. If we begin our theology of God's power by focusing on the way Jesus empowered people like Mary or Zacchaeus or the woman with the flow of blood, we cannot speak of a pattern of relationship where someone orders and the other obeys. Our covenant relationship with God has more to do with God's accepting our "personal autonomy" while continually inviting us into relationship. Living according to the covenant arises out of the empowerment and friendship which God offers to us.

3. *Our theology of cult and its role in restoring shalom when it is broken needs to focus more directly on feelings of anger and the notion of forgiveness if we want to include those who have been abused in our worship.* When we acknowledge that false guilt and false forgiveness are temptations of the one who has been abused, we will have to look more seriously at how we can legitimately express anger and pain in our worship settings. The psalms which express anger and even wish for vengeance have often been an embarrassment to Mennonite peace theology. We do not know how to incorporate them into our worship experience. However, when trust is broken, when justice has not been done, when the temple has been violated, the faith community will need to incorporate ways to express anger into their common life. They will have to find a process which does not begin with quick superficial forgiveness but wrestles with the gravity of sin. This will have to be done in a way that places the community into the presence of God who brings shalom to our relationships.

4. *The cross as a major symbol of the power of God in making shalom will need to be re-examined in order to understand its role in the life of someone who is abused.* The way of the cross as suffering

love looks different if we speak from the standpoint of someone who feels powerless in the face of the abuser.

Perhaps a direction in which to go is to look at the disciples and their struggle with the cross. This would mean to focus on both male and female disciples and their struggle to follow Jesus. What was the challenge that Jesus gave to those who felt particularly powerless? Was the way of the cross the same for those who felt weak and inconsequential as for those who felt a sense of worth and authority? What do we make of the failures of the disciples and the response of Jesus to them?

We may also want to explore new aspects of Jesus as model. For example, we can gain a new sense of the need for empowerment when we focus on the times when Jesus needed the support of his friends, when he struggled in Gethsemane for a sense of purpose in the senseless violence around him, when he needed to be strengthened and empowered before he could go the way of suffering love.

Another direction that needs further exploration is to look again at the differences between the cross of Jesus and the suffering of those who experience violence and abuse. Are they really the same? What makes suffering redemptive? Where does resurrection fit in the theology of suffering?

I have indicated a few directions that a Mennonite peace theology would need to explore if we began to listen to the voices of those who have been silenced or marginalized in our family conversations.

Perhaps we can think of biblical theology as an exercise in "home-making." However, this home-making is not reserved for only one person who is given a role of house-keeping so that everything will be neat and tidy. Instead all of us must become involved in the vital conversation process which does not cover up injustice or abuse in the home but instead deals with them in a healing way. It is then that we will discover anew the Source of Love who is the center of our home, our God who has given birth to us, suffered with us in our lack of shalom, challenged us in our injustice and empowered us anew to live the way of love in a violent world.

NOTES

    1. Walter Brueggeman speaks of biblical interpretation as "home-making" in his book *Interpretation and Obedience* (Minneapolis: Fortress, 1991), 8. Note also the way he uses the metaphor of God and the people of God as home-makers in chapter 13, "Welcoming the Stranger," 290-310.

Chapter 2

REDEMPTIVE RESISTANCE TO VIOLATION OF WOMEN: CHRISTIAN POWER, JUSTICE, AND SELF-GIVING LOVE

Gayle Gerber Koontz

While I do not work professionally with abused women, like all of us with eyes to see and ears to hear, violence to and violation of women touches my life regularly.

- Several weeks ago a seminary student reported that a niece in Zimbabwe was taken forcefully from her first husband by a former boyfriend who then married her, and after several years and having begun a family, brutally murdered her with a knife.

- A female student from the Mennonite high school in Goshen was raped and murdered last January.

- Within the past year a member of my congregation has begun to speak more openly about the incest she experienced as a child.

- A former student from Canada reported that her uncles used to pay 25 cents to fondle their neices; when the girls told their aunts, the aunts looked the other way.

- I know personally at least three Mennonite pastors and church leaders (and am aware of others) who resigned or were terminated because of breaking appropriate sexual boundaries with persons in their care.

I would like to explore here one Christian response to violence against women, an ethic which I have attempted to characterize in the phrase "redemptive resistance to evil." I will outline what I see as the theological foundations for this ethic with special reference to God's power in the face of evil. It is an exploratory position, perhaps a controversial one, but hopefully one which will nudge us to some further conversation. Following the theological-ethical material I will make some suggestions about what accepting an ethic of redemptive resistance to violence against women might mean for Christian perpetrators, Christian survivors of violence and abuse, and Christian neighbors of both.

Some of you may be aware of the 1991 Mennonite Central Committee publication, *Mennonite Peace Theology: A Panorama of Types*, edited by J. R. Burkholder and Barbara Nelson Gingerich.[1] In that booklet ten different types of Mennonite approaches to peace

theology are initially identified. They share in common the rejection
of lethal violence as an option for Anabaptist believers. All of them
claim the authority of Scripture and all posit the church community
as a primary loyalty. The position I will describe today stands in that
stream.

Among types of Mennonite peace theology, if one must be
forced into a typology, my own thinking and work related to violence
against women is perhaps closest to what is there called "liberation
pacifism." Issues of justice and taking into account the reality of
power have been important for Mennonite peace theology, at least
since the 1960s. There has been increasing concern that peace be
defined not simply by apparent or surface harmony (absence of
violence), but as rooted in fundamentally just and loving relations.
Liberation pacifism is clearly interested in peace with justice and is
concerned to stand in solidarity with the poor, the oppressed, and
the suffering.

There is some debate in *Mennonite Peace Theology* about
whether Mennonites inclined toward liberation pacifism tend to
emphasize justice more than peace and whether they truly accept
nonviolence as a norm for Christian ethics. Some of the issues that

are discussed in this context are: Can pacifism be a meaningful
option for Christians in situations that seem to call for revolutionary
change? Isn't pacifism finally passive, being a quiet co-conspirator in
violence, a form of giving in to the status quo? Doesn't such a commitment finally mean abandoning those who are suffering from
death-dealing oppression? How can a relatively powerful Christian
pacifist share peace convictions in relationship with relatively powerless people who are bearing the brunt of suffering?

Liberation pacifists have also been sensitive to how differences in power affect theological and ethical vision. There is the
recognition that theology and ethics developed by people of privilege
and power often do not speak to the reality of the relatively powerless. There are attempts therefore to identify emphases which make
sense not only to the relatively powerful, but also to those with much
lesser power. However, Mennonites who have begun to write with
liberation justice in mind have not given very much attention to
women-men relationships as an area of injustice. There is room for
further creative work here.

In thinking about liberation pacifism in relation to violence
against women, I have chosen to speak of "redemptive resistance to
violence toward and violation of women." I have chosen those words
carefully because words carry freight.

Violence. In the light of larger peace theology discussions, I
believe it is helpful in our moral discourse to make some distinction

between violence and violation. It allows us to distinguish a particular form of coercion: physical coercion. I will use the term "violence" to refer to situations when physical coercion or force is used to assail a woman sexually or otherwise. Almost all such violence toward adult women is done by men. However, as Vange Willms Thiessen points out, it is simplistic to blame only men for the problem. In parenting, both women and men contribute to the development and socialization of men who express violence toward women and of women who accept it as natural or normal.[2]

Violation. I will use the term "violation" when other than physical forms of coercion or pressure--such as emotional, economic, psychological, or social--are used to exploit or harm women. This is an almost unmanageably broad category, but it includes some situations that may be of particular interest to us here, for example, some cases of incest or of breaking appropriate sexual boundaries between pastors and counselees, or professors and students, when the woman involved *apparently* assents or consents to sexual activity so that physical coercion is not needed.

The difference is not that violence involves the body and violation the spirit. Both violence and violation involve body and spirit. The distinction is whether physical coercion or force (violence) or other forms of coercion (violation) are involved.

In Christian perspective both violence and violation are sin. Both make relationships characterized by Christ-like love impossible. They feed fear, self-hatred, hostility, endemic suspicion, secrecy and isolation, and prevent families, congregations and communities from being places where God's peaceable rule exists-- where there is safety, security, justice, and well-being.

It also seems to me that violence is not by definition a more serious sin than violation. It is important for us to identify this, particularly in Mennonite contexts where we have focused on the rejection of physical force. Some forms of violation may be even more serious or harmful than some forms of violence. For example, a situation of incest where a child is not physically coerced or a situation between an employer and an employee where there is sexual activity without physical coercion but where the power relationship is dramatically unequal, may be more profoundly damaging to the individual, family, and community than a man hitting and knocking down a woman in a domestic fight (violence) where the women retains some significant powers in relation to the man.

Redemptive. The peace ethic I will be developing assumes God's underlying love and compassion and offer of healing to survivors of violence and forgiveness to assailants. It affirms that God empowers as well as forgives. We are not stuck, limited to destructive behaviors or to hostility toward enemies. There is the possibility of renewed life for walking in the light of Christ. "Redemptive" affirms a Mennonite-Christian tradition of compassionate response to those who suffer, transformation and discipleship through grace, and a missionary love of enemy.

Resistance, not Passivity. Redemptive "resistance" means rejection of an understanding of nonresistance that implies doing nothing in the face of violence or evil. While I do not think that its serious proponents have seen nonresistance as doing nothing, a truncated view that equates passivity and nonresistance is tragically inadequate. Those who work with women who are being battered testify to cases where women accept violence against them partly because they believe they are to submit to their husbands and to turn the other cheek.

Redemptive resistance is not an ethic of passivity in the face of evil. The language of resistance highlights this in a way similar to those who within Mennonite peace theology have begun to speak of nonviolent resistance rather than nonresistance. But the debate about nonviolent resistance versus nonresistance is also related to the question of whether and to what degree we recognize and accept the use of coercion other than physical force in our response to evil.

It seems to me there are three basic trajectories available to us in relation to identified "enemies." They are: 1) violent resistance; 2) nonviolent coercive resistance (which includes adopting forms of coercive or controlling action other than physical coercion; and 3) persuasive resistance (which seeks to resist evil acts without controlling or coercing the perpetrators).

I will further explore the third trajectory, an ethic committed to persuasive forms of resistance to evil because it fits best with my Mennonite, though not exclusively Mennonite, reading of Jesus, and given that standing point, my understanding of the character and purposes of God and my understandings of Christian pacifism. While my theology is trinitarian, I have chosen, if understandings of God and the Holy Spirit seem to conflict for some reason with understandings focused in Jesus, to give preference to understandings based on Jesus. These commitments assume that the biblical witness to Christ is normatively formative for Christian theology and ethics and they are based on my understanding of what it means to call oneself Christian. There are other choices, but in my view choosing to be Christian implies these directions.

Secondly, I continue to lament the ravaging of the weak of the earth, of women, which occurs when dominating power, the use of violence and coercion, is claimed and used for the good of some rather than for the good of the whole. My proposal is that Christians must relinquish dominating power itself, not only the ends toward which it may be directed. In this view dominating power is not only contrary to God's own exercise of power, but it does not lead to the creation of the kind of world community that God intends, whether employed by power holders or by those who have been broken by them.

An ethic of redemptive resistance is rooted in theological convictions about God's grace, justice, and power. God is just. God's power is directed toward justice on earth. God attends to those who are marginalized and suffer from systems and attitudes of injustice, liberating them from self-hatred, isolation, bondage, and despair. God's judgment, God's light cuts through self-deception, human excuse, corrupt systems, and violated relationships, showing their failure in relation to God's purposes on earth and dramatically underlining the need for repentance. God is just.

God is also loving. Freely choosing to draw near to humans, God profoundly loves creation and is compassionate toward those who need healing. God is merciful, patient, forgiving of individuals and communities who truly repent and turn toward God. God's compassion makes it possible for victims of violence to be empowered for new life, and for enemies of God to become friends of God. God is loving.

God's power, evident in the life, death, and resurrection of Jesus, resists evil by judgment, noncooperation, creating alternative options and paths, empowering the weak, sustaining hope through suffering, healing and renewing life--even through death--but not by violent or clearly coercive resistance to powers which seek to dominate those whose faith rests in Christ and God.

In the phrase "redemptive resistance" to evil I refer to an ethic which assumes that Christians are called and empowered by God to follow the example of Jesus in seeking justice and loving God, our neighbors, and our enemies. I affirm therefore a traditional Mennonite emphasis on self-giving love and love of enemy. I also affirm Christian concern for and action to bring about just relations among people on earth, particularly between women and men. Resisting the evil of violence toward and violation of women includes a positive call to both women and men to attend to power in their relationships, to work toward redirecting that power for the good of both, and to advocate balancing their powers as a foundation for mutuality and friendship within the household of God.

One dimension of this kind of peace theology, which I think requires further attention, has to do with God's power. How we understand power as peace church people is critical, it seems to me, for drawing together the claims that God is both loving and just, and for holding together coherently a Christian ethic that is both pacifist and committed to liberation from the sins of sexism and violence to women.

Anna Case-Winters in a 1990 book, *God's Power: Traditional Understandings and Contemporary Challenges,* suggests there are two fundamentally different ways of understanding power. The first one she calls "power in the mode of domination and control." Such power seeks "to exercise restraint upon the free action of, to hold sway over, to exercise power or authority over; to dominate, command; hold in check, curb, restrain from action, hinder, prevent; to overpower, overmaster, overrule."[3] Domination conveys the personal nature of control. It is rooted in the word "dominus" which means lord or master. It is this meaning of power which for many theologians underlies the traditional doctrine of omnipotence--the effectual exercise of the divine personal will in accomplishing divine purposes.

The second definition of power, based on the work of Charles Hartshorne, is "the capacity to influence and be influenced." It is persuasive in this sense, rather than coercive. "Power of influence," Case-Winters writes, "is always power within limits."[4] Power in this definition may dramatically influence, but does not control. In contrast to a tradition which assigns all freedom and power to God, this view sees freedom and power as essential to every subject. God is unique in that God has the power to influence all and is influenced by all.

This second view of power, it seems to me, is consistent with God's creative power visible through Jesus and with the work of the Holy Spirit. God's power seen in the life, death and resurrection of Jesus is power which preserves and redeems. God through Christ resists, heals, and transforms evil, but refuses to control or dominate others in the process. It is compatible with a Christian peace church interpretation of Scripture.

Further, such an understanding of power clearly affirms human freedom and responsibility in relation to divine power. The theological tradition which depends on the first definition tends to equivocate on power and freedom. When God controls the way things are, we have difficulty trying to make sense of human freedom and moral responsibility. A foundational understanding of God's power as persuasive power maximizes human freedom within limits, making freely responsive love and action possible and meaningful. Divine power, evident in the cross as well as in Jesus' life and resurrection, preserves our freedom as women and men to reject dramatically God's own will and way. The quality of God's relationship to us is marked by vulnerability and respect.

Persuasive power also promotes an ethic of reciprocity or mutual responsibility rather than an ethic of obedience. Case-Winters argues that when power in the mode of domination and control is ascribed to God, it is elevated and in the process legitimated for ethics for human relations. Maintaining control (presumably for the good of the whole) and being obedient to those in authority become primary virtues. When persuasive power is elevated and reenacted in human affairs by those with authority, it does not have the same damaging social consequences as dominating power.

The understanding of power as the capacity to influence and be influenced focuses and legitimates the notion of power within respectful relationships and the exercise of power in cooperation with other powers. It undergirds the notion of empowering as opposed to overpowering. It is compatible with commitment to mutuality in decision-making.

We may for these reasons give primacy to persuasive power. But in the face of profound evil, is it a strong enough power? Where does divine justice come in? Suffering, including violence and violation borne by women, raises that nagging question: How can we trust the goodness and power of a God who does not use violent or coercive power to resist evil, when there is so much relentless violation and suffering? We preach and teach and seek to emulate the love and compassion of God ("Father, forgive them for they know not what they do"), wondering, in our heart of hearts, what it means to say that compassionate, redemptive love is powerful before profound evil.

THE POWER OF COMPASSION

Wendy Farley, a theologian from Emory, has taught me a great deal about one form of redemptive love--compassion. She argues that compassion is powerful. "Compassion is power to bring to life what is broken by pain, to bring to justice and redemption what is twisted by brutality, to free creatures from the torment of self-absorption and enliven them for care, delight, and creativity."[5] But just how is this power powerful? How does it resist evil?

On the one hand compassion resists evil because it is a power which influences rather than forces. In this sense, it opposes itself to the evil of dominating power. Compassionate love, contrary to popular belief, is not helpless before force. It resists force more thoroughly even than counter-force, because it refuses to accept the claim that dominating power is the strongest or ultimate power. As soon as one fights dominating power with dominating power one has given in to its claim to be the strongest power on earth. Farley writes that compassion recognizes that it is not possible to resist a world order based on dominance on its own terms. "One must repudiate the desire for domination: this in itself is the heart of the struggle against evil."[6]

Compassion represents a different type of desire and power. Compassion seems to be, Farley writes, "the power that holds out longest against evil."[7] In this view Jesus' compassion at the cross for his executioners is not nonresistance but ultimate resistance. In this sense it is the final and thoroughgoing repudiation of the power of domination and terror. It refuses to respond to domination and terror by trying to dominate in return, by refusing to return evil with evil.

It is one thing, however, for a Christian to choose this path of resistance to evil for herself. It is one thing for me to say, "Given my vision of God and ethical commitments, if someone were to try to violate me, I choose to walk the path of redemptive resistance." It is quite another to stand by while other women are beaten, raped, and violated. It is this point--the suffering of the innocent--that has plagued pacifists from the beginning. And it is at this point that the just war tradition offers powerful arguments to justify use of violence. Does not repudiation of the desire for domination and its attending powers mean passivity in the face of evil?

Emptying oneself of the power to dominate is *not* emptying oneself of power. Emptying oneself of the power to dominate makes room for the powers of preservation and redemption. And one of those powers, compassion, does not stand by passively while evil violates the weak. Compassion is powerful, not only because it resists the desire and power of domination itself, but because it is a power which helps people who are suffering claim their own power. It overcomes dependence, despair, and powerlessness. This is key for those of us who function as helping professionals and pastors in relation to violated women.

Compassion is empowering. How is that? Farley suggests four ways.[8] First, compassion gives dignity to sufferers, the humiliated. The difference between pity and compassion is that compassion does not simply feel sorry for, but respects the sufferer. Compassion is sympathetic knowledge of suffering that mediates dignity to the sufferer. "To receive compassion is to receive respect." Receiving respect helps to restore self-respect. In this way compassion "becomes an agency to resist the effects of suffering."[9] Compassion empowers.

Violated women frequently suffer from low self-esteem, even self-hatred. They have not been respected. I am reminded of Brenda and Janice, Mennonite Central Committee workers who spent several years befriending hospitality women (prostitutes) in Olangapo City in the Philippines. Brenda and Jan began visiting bars, listening and building relationships with violated women. To women who regularly subjected themselves to various degrading forms of sexual practices and gave themselves to relationships in which their trust and their hopes were frequently betrayed, Brenda and Jan offered respect. Slowly the women were empowered to begin to speak about the pain of their lives and to claim dignity in relation to these American foreign church women.

Second, compassion mediates courage to resist the causes of suffering. Compassion by nurturing self-respect among the violated gives rise to new visions for relationships, characterized by justice and fairness. Compassion inspires individuals in communities to resist the degrading effects of suffering and to defy structures and policies that institutionalize injustice. Compassion also mediates the courage to confront personal guilt. In this sense compassion seeks and empowers for justice.

Some of the Filipino hospitality women began to talk more together, partly as a result of Brenda and Jan's quietly finding out who knew whom and encouraging connections. Eventually the women joined to find a space, a small building where they could come together. First they invited resource people to teach them about health care. Later they assisted each other with "night care" for their children while they were at work, and developed ways to educate guests from other parts of the Philippines and the world about the linkages between prostitution and the U.S. military presence in the community. Slowly, often with frustrating failures, the women began to realize their power, however small, in standing together in the face of the suspicion of bar owners and local government.

Third, compassion resists the power of suffering to dominate sufferers. It directs itself against inevitable or hopeless suffering, suffering that can not be effectively resisted. Compassion is a form of comfort and strength when it does not seem realistic to hope that suffering will end. The situation of the women in Olongapo was very complex. In overall perspective it was difficult to see how there would be any possibility for systematic transformation and change. (The U.S. decision to remove its bases was not perceived as likely at the time.) Redemption in such a situation lies in "the capacity of the sufferer to still taste the presence of divine love even through the torment. In the midst of suffering, redemptive power is present to prevent it from stealing a final victory. Even in hopelessness there is resistance to the destructive power of suffering."[10]

Compassion can empower sufferers by breaking the dominion of suffering over the spirit. Divine compassion and its expression in the compassion of others offers comfort and strength to battered spirits.

In Olongapo Brenda and Jan often wept at suffering that seemed impossible to effectively resist. One young woman's foreign client left a vibrator inside her. She later died from resulting infection. Brenda and Jan noted in amazement the expressions of courage and compassion which the hospitality women, some of them self-consciously Christian, continued to show to each other and to Brenda and Jan in the midst of what seemed to be a hopeless cycle of violence and violation. I suspect that Brenda's and Jan's genuine compassion, motivated by God's compassion, also played a role in helping to crack the dominion of suffering over the women they learned to love.

Finally, compassion mediates the power of redemption. Compassion which recognizes and responds to the dignity and sorrow of sinners, mediates healing power. It can restore hope and vitality. Divine compassion is directed not only to those who are dominated and battered in spirit, but extends to sinners and enemies of God. The "annoying and insulting thing about compassion," Farley writes, "is it seems to be too soft-hearted.... Divine mercy permits outrage over wickedness to be accompanied by redemption from sin."[11] God condemns evil by redeeming the one who does evil, and in this way destroys evil. Redemption, though, requires that one see and repent of the evil one is responsible for before guilt can be overcome. Redemptive compassion does not renew suffering or repudiate judgment, but indicates that guilt is not the final word. Even for the prophets, whom we associate with judgment, "wrath was rarely more than a heartbeat away from mercy."[12]

Divine compassion. Divine compassion is powerful, but because it refuses to use power for domination, it cannot coerce. It is a condition of redemption. It mediates healing power, but it does not determine a response. Compassion is an offer, a presence. It occurs in the context of relationship and is contingent upon response. Therefore, compassion can be frustrated by sin, by injustice and it is in that sense, vulnerable or weak. The failure of compassion, however, lies not in its impotence or powerlessness, but in its relational context. But this is also its value and strength. Compassion "respects the uniqueness and beauty of every creature and opens the space for each one to delight and work and create for itself and community with others. It is through the guise of weak-

ness that compassion gives to creatures their own strength."[13]
    Because of its vulnerability there are enormous risks in engaging the power of compassion in the serious struggle against dominating power. While it is possible to cite many stories about the transforming power of compassion,[14] such power is not guaranteed to win the struggle in a particular time and place, nor does God promise that in serious attempts to resist evil we will avoid death. There is a certain "abandon that is proper to compassion," Farley says, "an abandon that must be grounded in trust."[15] In the overall story of this planet, God's redemptive love is the final power, not violent power or death. That is the eschatological hope and choice. God can be trusted to bring fidelity, justice, and well-being together, for God is here and now a God of power.

ETHICS FOR THE POWERFUL AND THE WEAK

    What does this kind of theological and ethical vision imply for Christian response to violence against and violation of women specifically? I do not think we can respond to that question generically. Redemptive resistance to evil seems to imply different things depending on one's relational standing point--whether one is or has been a victim/survivor, an abuser, or a neighbor of an abuser or victim. It is important to distinguish between ethics for relatively powerful sinners who violate others, for relatively powerless victims or survivors, and for relatively powerful neighbors of both (all of us fit at least this category). Redemptive resistance to evil might serve as a normative ethical framework for each, but the specific moral responsibilities (and the theological emphases appealed to in undergirding them) might be quite different for abusers, survivors, and neighbors. For example, an abuser who professes to be a Christian must resist the habit, desire, and need to control, and must let go of dominating power in relation to others, especially in relation to women. He needs a theological and personal reorientation which connects power with masculine servanthood and self-giving love. A victim, on the other hand, usually needs to claim her power to act and to develop a sense of self and its value. In this case a theological and personal reorientation that emphasizes God's love for women, desire for justice, care for the suffering, and empowerment of the weak and marginalized is critical. For neighbors of those who inflict and those who suffer violence and violation, ethics are also relationship dependent and include a range of responsibilities from offering protection and healing presence to the violated, to speaking the truth in love to violators and offering forgiveness to the repentant.

Trying to develop this further apart from specific cases is difficult since different contextual factors need to be taken into consideration: whether the violence or violation is taking place in an ongoing relationship or was a one time incident; whether it is current or past; whether we are talking about violence or violation and to what extent; whether the victim or survivor has extremely limited power, a very little sense of self, little or no supportive community, or greater degrees of one or more of those factors. Given this complexity, my remaining comments need to be taken as rough strokes. They need to be tested, evaluated, refined and reshaped in relation to various concrete situations of violence to and violation of women.

I will comment first on Christian ethics for the relatively weak, survivors, or potential victims. In this case redemptive resistance is directed outward to the sources of violence and violation. Acts of resistance in this case need to be appropriate to persons with limited power. There are special situations, such as childhood incest, where victims simply do not have power. In such cases an ethic of redemptive resistance does not apply; a child who does not have the power to act does not bear moral responsibility. Neither does such an ethic apply to women who have not chosen the Christian way of peace. But assuming there is at least some power available to most adult women in North American society, Christian survivors and potential victims are ethically responsible to use this power in response to evil. To what degree then, we need to ask, do specific survivors or victims have power? If the weak have power to resist, then what kinds of available resistance are compatible with the ethical position I have outlined?

My leaning, of course, is toward redemptive or persuasive, rather than coercive forms of resistance.

1) *Refusing to despair.* Despair is the end of hope and the beginning of paralysis. Hope is a gift of God and of others. It is a commitment. It can be nurtured.

2) *Fleeing.* There is significant historical Mennonite precedence for this response!

3) *Covert resistance.* Last summer I saw the *Martyrs Mirror* exhibition which included some dramatic examples of covert resistance. Women have been creative in this area in the past. It might be a step for economically dependent battered women or victims of sexual harassment.

4) *Breaking silence and seeking help.* This is often critical for battered women and victims of incest and sexual harassment. Choosing to trust compassionate others, rather than standing alone is a significant act of resistance. This includes seeking psychological, emotional and pastoral healing.

5) *Saying no to perpetrators of violence or violation.* It is possible in abusive marriage situations, that saying no might lead to divorce or in situations of sexual violation by an employer, to loss of job. If a victim has a strong enough sense of self, and depending on the extent of violation and the attitude of the violator, in some cases resistance might take the form of making sexual and personal boundaries very clear while continuing to offer relationship or friendship.

All of these actions resist violence or violation without inflicting violence. At the same time all of them, except the very last, can be taken with great bitterness toward the perpetrator. In Christian ethical and pastoral perspective, an ethic of *redemptive* resistance includes at some point a dimension of compassionate response on the part of the victim or survivor in relation to the perpetrator of violence. Compassion does not mean that a survivor does not feel angry. It does mean that redemption and forgiveness of the abuser is part of the agenda for a Christian victim. However if one considers the pyschological and spiritual steps that are proposed for women recovering from violent assault and violation, forgiveness is rather far down on the list.

In pastoral perspective I do not think that we should expect Christian victims to *feel* forgiveness immediately, or perhaps even after a very long time. However in ethical perspective, I believe it is important for Christian survivors to *act* immediately according to the norm of enemy love. At this point I would draw on the distinction between feeling and doing. That is, a survivor may not *feel* forgiving, but she should not *retaliate* with violent or revengeful acts. I would argue in the same way that while Christian perpetrators may not necessarily *feel* sorry immediately, it is urgent that they *act* according to the norms of justice and love. They should stop harming and not ask the one who they violated for anything, including asking for immediate forgiveness.

In spite of what I have indicated so far, I do recognize that there are some hard cases where there seem to be no actions consistent with persuasive or even nonviolent power that would protect the victims. Is there ever a time when a violent course of resistance is acceptable in response to violence against women? In essence this is the familiar argument, "Wouldn't you hit someone over the head-- or kill--if they were going to shoot your grandmother?" In the past I struggled with this for a long time and after listening to hosts of arguments decided that it is not wise to let the hard cases determine our basic ethical orientation. Such cases are usually not the ones we face. In many more cases, persuasive resistance can have effect, sometimes dramatic effect. It is my conviction that our energies

would be better spent focusing on how a peace ethic applies in the
majority of situations where persusasive power might be transformative and in actually using persuasive resistance to work preventively
so that genuinely hard cases occur less often.

I do not mean to wriggle out of addressing hard cases
altogether, but rather to set them in perspective. Hard cases are
inherently tragic. There is no way to justify violence, it seems to me,
either on the part of the one who is inflicting it or the suffering one
who retaliates with it. Such situations are simply and profoundly
tragic. In response to such situations, we should weep.

At the same time I would point out that the trajectory in
which I have moved in this paper suggests that if there is the choice,
and if one adopts an ethic of redemptive resistance, it is not
appropriate for a victim or survivor to inflict violence on the
assailant. I do not say this lightly. I hear and respect the passion in
the voice of a woman who has been raped saying, "I would rather kill
or be killed than be raped again." I have heard and respect the passion in African-American voices emerging from personal memories
of bodies hanging from trees. Many among the latter, certainly during the period of slavery, chose silence and survival. Some chose
violent resistance against the evil of racism. A number also consciously chose paths of redemptive resistance. It is my conviction
that this path is the most consistent with Christian faith as I best
understand it.

Not all ethical options are live options for any individual.
Redemptive resistance, for example, requires a certain theological
vision and perhaps community. But for those like myself who have
adopted consciously and intentionally a theological vision like that I
have described and who have chosen to be part of a Christian community of peace, it seems to me that the path of redemptive
resistance is the most consistent one. For me this includes choosing
not to use violence, even were I to be violated.

One small but controversial example here is a Christian
woman's use of nonlethal violence in relation to self-defense. A
woman is in danger in our society. Current statistics indicate that
one in four women are likely to be assaulted. That is a frightening
statistic. Research also shows that a woman is in danger in our
society, not just from strangers but among friends and
acquaintances. Vulnerable women sometimes need to go out at
night. Should we carry cans of mace in our purses? I consciously do
not. Yet in a context where fears continue to be fed by violent incidents, the justification of violent resistance is tempting.

The argument that it is better to spray mace in someone's
eyes and prevent him from raping me because that keeps him from

sinning and me from harm appears persuasive. Yet I wonder if we see clearly the connections between this kind of logic and the logic of justifying war which we have sought to repudiate as a peace church. And there is the rub. Just war thinking also justifies the use of violence to protect the innocent, maybe even for the good of the aggressor. Just war thinking distinguishes between discriminate and indiscriminate use of violence, justifying violence when it is clearly directed at a known aggressor and rejecting it when innocents are indiscriminately harmed. While the use of mace is of a very different scale than using arms in the context of war, the logic of justification is similar. The use of mace would be discriminate use of violence clearly directed at a known aggressor.

In spite of the way I have framed this question so far, I believe that pacifist commitment to redemptive resistance is not primarily a negative act (rejection of violence) but a creative act (leaving an opening for the transforming power of God). The alternative to carrying mace is not passive cooperation in being violated. I know one pacifist woman who carries a piercing whistle. Another refers to an ethical framework in which the safety of both the assailant and the victim are kept in mind, pressing her to imagine and practice nonthreatening responses to an assailant but also responses which quickly and clearly assert her personhood when she is being treated as an object.[16]

Redemptive resistance attempts to recall, value, and promote the character of individuals and communities marked by trust, gentleness, strength, courage, risk, loyalty, and compassion--virtues born of love for, faith and trust in the God described above. Can you imagine one of the fleeing evangelical Anabaptists kicking a pursuer in the groin? Resting one's sense of security in violent forms of self-defense seems to me to be part of a journey other than the one which has guided those who founded and sustained our peace church tradition. Is Dirk Willems--the Anabaptist martyr who stopped to save his pursuer who had fallen through the ice--wrongheaded or a profoundly compelling example of Christian ethics? It is a choice we must make. It is not an easy choice.

Redemptive resistance for abusers. For the relatively powerful, for abusers who profess to be Christian, resistance must be directed inwardly toward the violence which they have committed or may commit. The most urgent ethical requirement is to stop the violent behavior. It can never be justified. Such a person must seek psychological-emotional healing, commit himself to resist future sins of violence against women and work against internal and external pressures to exercise controlling power. Recognizing one's own power in relation to women considering the cultural context and one's social role, not simply considering whether one *feels* powerful overall is essential. Women must not be used as scapegoats for the powerlessness one feels in relation to other men, economic realities, etc. Accountability to other Christians--pastor, counselor, elder--for continuing resistance is helpful and necessary. One who stands as a relatively powerful person in a trust relationship with a female--father-daughter, teacher-student, employer-employee, pastor-member of church, counselor-client--must take care not to sexualize the relationship or cross sexual boundaries even when the women seems to assent, resisting using one's power to make fantasy actuality. Marie Fortune's work, Peter Rutter's *Sex in the Forbidden Zone*, and Karen Lebacqz' and Ronald Barton's *Sex in the Parish* elucidate these emphases. Redemptive resistance repents of the sin before God, before other Christians, and if possible before the survivor. Forgiveness from God and from representatives of the Christian church must be sought but not expected from the survivor.

Redemptive resistance for neighbors of survivors and abusers. Those who stand in third party relationships, as Christian neighbors to survivors and abusers, are called to claim God's redemptive power and mediate God's judgment and love. Christian neighbors have the responsibility to communicate to both survivors and abusers what the two have not and may not be able to communicate to one another: you are valuable and lovable in God's eyes.

In relation to victims/survivors, neighbors can mediate the power of compassion and stand in solidarity. In crisis ministries, neighbors can listen, hold, weep, and provide safe and accepting spaces. In longer term relationships, neighbors can work for the empowerment of victims by being trustworthy, offering respect, helping survivors connect with other survivors, helping make practical alternatives to ongoing suffering possible, being available to receive and respond to religious dimensions of experiences of violation, standing in solidarity when survivors act to say "no more violence."

In relation to assailants or perpetrators, neighbors can take personal risk in confronting abusers regarding specific actions of violence toward or violation of women. Neighbors can speak the truth in love, offering compassion that can enable repentance and personal structures of accountability that undergird and support genuine change.

Christian communities can offer special, preventive ministry to men in this culture. James Nelson indicates that men in this culture find it extremely difficult to say, "I need, I hurt, and I can't." This has to do with power, with being socialized into a male role which assumes that taking control in relationships is an important part of male identity. Preaching and teaching an understanding of

God that celebrates persuasive power and being a worshipping and acting community that makes it possible for men to admit, "I need, I hurt, I can't" and to still value them and accept them as men of strength and spirit can be a profound ministry in a culture which values male control. It is a way to resist cultural patterns which contribute to violence against women and to provide redemptive space for men to grow in faithfulness to Christ, to women, and to other men.[17]

A former seminary faculty member suggests a more Mennonite trilogy than Nelson. First, the importance for men, and thereby for women, of the love of God and of enemy love for harnessing aggressiveness. Second, the importance of grace through Christ and of transformative justice which can lead a community to solve problems in a peaceable, mutual way rather than in an adversarial way. And third, the importance of the community of the Holy Spirit which calls men away from the radical individualism and loneliness which often characterizes relationships among men in this society and contributes to emotional dynamics in men-women relationships.[18]

In relation to both survivors and perpetrators of violence against women, Christian neighbors have options for further action. There are possibilities for education about and critique of the cultural or religious ethos, assumptions and power relations which undergird violence to women, dimensions which Ruth Krall underlines in her paper. Neighbors can pursue legal and social change toward more equal distribution of power between women and men.[19] Perhaps most profoundly, Christian neighbors can commit ourselves to live according to, and thereby witness to, the possibility of mutuality. Here I share with Mary Schertz the sense of the importance of the integrity of community life. Rather than living by patterns of the domination and subordination of women by men in our families and congregations, we can provide hope by example of a social structure for counter-cultural living. We can preach, teach, and worship and live to the glory of a powerfully, creative, redemptive, just, and compassionate God.

NOTES

1. J. R. Burkholder, and Barbara Nelson Gingerich. *Mennonite Peace Theology: A Panorama of Types*. Akron, Pa.: Mennonite Central Committee, 1991.

2. "Case Study on Domestic Violence: A Theology of Peace and a Theology of Liberation." Presented at the Peace Theology Colloquium, Vancouver, B.C., June 1991. Further, as Ruth Krall has developed for us, the problem of violence toward women is rooted in systemic cultural problems.

3. *Oxford English Dictionary*, cited in Case-Winters, (Louisville: Westminster, John Knox, 1990).

4. Case-Winters, 209.

5. Wendy Farley, *Tragic Vision and Divine Compassion: A Contemporary Theodicy*. (Louisville: Westminster, John Knox, 1990), 93.

6. Farley, 92. Art McGill also recognizes and makes this point in *Suffering: A Test of Theological Method*. (Philadelphia: Westminster, 1982). During the discussion at the consultation someone commented that Jesus suffered at the cross because he was *resisting* the powers. Nonresistance would have meant giving in and going along with what they wanted him to do, including giving up his ministry. It is important to interpret the meaning of the cross in the context of Jesus' life and resurrection and not in isolation.

7. Farley, 90.

8. *Ibid.*, 116-19.

9. *Ibid.*, 79, 80-81.

10. *Ibid.*, 117.

11. *Ibid.*, 119-120.

12. *Ibid.*, 123.

13. *Ibid.*, 94.

14. For example, see Cornelia Lehn's collection, *Peace Be With You*, (Newton, Kans.: Faith and Life Press, 1980), and Niall O'Brien, *Revolution from the Heart*, (New York: Oxford, 1987).

15. Farley, 84.

16. See Angie O'Gorman, "Defense Through Disarmament: Nonviolence and Personal Assault," in *The Universe Bends Toward Justice*, ed. Angie O'Gorman, (New Society Publishers, 1990). For a discussion of the practical application of martial arts in self-defense for women, see Pat James, "Physical Resistance to Attack: The Pacifist's Dilemma, The Feminist's Hope" and response by Pam McAllister, "Tentative Steps Toward Nonviolent Self-Defense" in *Reweaving the Web of Life*, ed. Pam McAllister, (New Society Press, 1982).

17. James Nelson, *The Intimate Connection*, (Philadelphia: Westminster Press, 1988).

18. These were suggested to me in a conversation with David Augsburger in September 1992.

19. Are not laws coercive and therefore to be repudiated by Christians seeking to follow paths of redemptive resistance? My too brief response is that law

provides structures within which orderly, loving, free human relations are possible. For human life to be ordered, there is always need for a legal structure. The question is not whether there are to be community laws or norms or not (unless one is an anarchist, which I am not) but which kinds of laws are most conducive to free and loving human relationships. Laws are not so much to force "offenders" to be a certain way as to provide structure for cooperative human relatedness.

RESPONSE

Lois J. Edmund

Thank you, Gayle, for your thoughtful paper and for your systematic attention and commitment to exploring this "touchy" subject. Active pacifism is difficult and has become muddled, and you have brought us a long way toward clarity.

I appreciate your positive approach of *liberation pacifism*. You affirm that as pacifists, we can act with purpose, can listen to, take direction from and work alongside the powerless in creating justice. Liberation pacifism can allow the relatively powerless to guide our theology and our redemptive action. This might help us concretely redirect and rebalance power. You remind us that if we as a theological community commit ourselves to resist all violence in interpersonal relationships, we might discover *redemptive resistance*. We can have hope for change and transformation if we can accept *compassion*. We must know the risks, and meet them bravely.

Gayle has acknowledged the importance of power which shapes and orders our relationships. I would like to turn our attention to power, and attempt a broader treatment.

Power is mysterious. In many ways it is intriguing and inviting, drawing us to gain it. In its vividness, power can be seductive. Men who are aware of their power report guilt and fear, but may not overcome lifelong power habits of denying "I need... I hurt... I can't" (James Nelson). Women often experience the sense of looking on to power, watching the powerful, waiting for "a turn."

Thelma Jean Goodrich (1991) identifies several important myths about power:

Myth #1: that power is "naturally" masculine, and that women do not and should not need power. In **actuality**, each of us, female and male, wants, needs and has power (or, at least, the benefits of power), but may have difficulty recognizing and admitting this.

Myth #2: that power is selfish and destructive, and that female possession of power will result in abandonment because it is unfeminine and unsexy. In **actuality**, power may be constructive or destructive, may be used obviously or underhandedly. Male and female fear of power, betrayed in this myth, obscures the sexuality of power, and the sexist power differential and its everyday consequences.

This morning, Lydia Harder (1991) identified a peculiarly Mennonite myth:

Myth #3: that powerlessness characterized Jesus' way. In **actuality** we have simply, naively idealized powerlessness, even Jesus' way, without understanding it, while fearing weakness and doing our best to hide it.

PSYCHOLOGY OF POWER

It would help us to assume that power simply is, and try to analyze it for better insight.
1. Power, and probably an inequity of power, exists in every human relationship.
2. Power is always exercised; it does not exist in static form. Power may be exercised with or without another's consent, unconsciously, habitually, subtly or overtly, but always in an interpersonal interaction.
3. Power is dynamic and emergent. Authentic interactions change daily and so will the possessors and users, as well as uses and balances of power.
4. Thus, power is always personal. Power cannot be removed from the possessor and his/her role and status. Power has to do with access: who participates in what activities, when, and in what ways. Persons cannot deny that they possess power.

We must not minimize the bad news about power. Power is seductive. Power can be destructive. Power is abused. All of us have the potential for using our existing power for ourselves and against good.

DEFINING POWER

It is difficult even to find consensus on the meaning of power. Gayle, with Case-Winters (1988), identified two modes: dominating power and persuading power. I think we can refine this even more. In the literature, we can find at least four understanding of power:

1. Power-over, might, dominating power. This is the reigning understanding of power, both in theological and in secular societies. Power is defined as might, strength, the prerogative to determine what happens. Although interactions may take the form of persuasion, influence, domination or control, in its essence this is coercive power which makes others yield to our will. Relationships are hierarchical, with each participant employing more, or less, power over every other participant. The power*ful* are those who enjoy authority, privilege, responsibility and control. The power*less* are those whose obligation it is to obey and, inevitably, to attempt to get the power of the powerful. Thus, the powerful must use strength, often threaten violence, in order to maintain their influence. Power-over borrows power from underneath: the powerful are powerful because they "over-power" the powerless. With Gayle, I say that this power must be relinquished in any Christian relationship.

Theologically, God is usually portrayed as a victor or con-queror, having this type of power over sin, over death, over the peoples of the earth. For example, "[Christ] is the head of all rule and power...He disarmed the principalities and powers and made public example of them, triumphing over them in [God]" (Col. 2:10, 15). This concept effectively ignores the babe in the manger, the hungry and tired miracle-worker, and the man on the cross.

There is suffering in this power model. The powerful fear deposition, are anxious and guilty about exposure. The powerless lose the dignity of self-determination. They are often seen as caus-ing their own inferiority by weakness, laziness, neediness. In reality, their power of personhood is stolen by those over them.

2. Power-to, ability. Social scientists have rejected the might model and have defined power as the ability to be oneself, to accomplish and achieve, to use one's gifts in fully meaningful roles. This type of power requires competency, security and autonomy, as well as access to resources necessary for self-fulfillment. This model therefore acknowledges the role of society in giving its members power, but tends to see power as individually achieved. The power*ful* are those who achieve authentic, fulfilling, gifted autonomy. The power*less* are those whose potential is stifled. The suffering here is of diminished creativity, frustration of stunted growth. When this power goes awry, we experience loneliness and abandonment. The God of Psalms could possibly be interpreted as possessing this type of power, but this concept is usually neglected theologically.

3. Power-for, empowerment. This model of power corresponds best with Gayle's description of *compassion*. Power is used for another. It is benevolent and is asymmetrically used for another's good. One person enhances another's abilities and strengths. Power is used to create, to guard and to support another's growth and development. This might be called mother-power. For example, a very interesting theological image is found in the Deuteronomy where God is like a mother eagle, who stirs up her nest, flutters over her young, spreads her wings to catch them when they fall and carries them on her back while teaching them to fly (32:11).

The ethic of this power is self-giving to achieve a good greater than oneself. It resembles self-giving, other-absorbed love, in which one person may need to lose something in order to enhance the other. Its essence is chosen, voluntary, and it may be vitally pacifist. The power*ful* desire the enhancement of the other, discern the needs of the power*less* and provide for satisfaction of need, regardless of their own needs. When this power goes awry, it leads to sacrifice, martyrdom. The suffering is in the (voluntary) unfulfillment or loss of self.

4. Power-with, solidarity, power-in-relation. Power may be found in the gathering of a body, in partnership of mutual interdependency. Power, here, is the capacity to join with another. Power is shared, not granted, and is found in the together-struggle, in cooperative respect and comfort. Intimacy, committed connection and interaction around changing powers (skills) are necessary. The power*ful*, in this model, are the connected and interdependent ones who are aware of their own and others' vulnerability and need. The powerless are the marginalized, abandoned, disconnected or dys-connected ones. Suffering is caused by in-group/out-group behavior: the power of exclusion. Isaiah 43 gives us a wonderful theological image of this power: "Fear not...When you pass through waters, I will be with you...they shall not overwhelm you...for I am the Lord, your God, the Holy One of Israel, your Savior...You are precious in my eyes and honored, and I love you...Fear not for I am with you." Here, God allows divine longing and delight in human company, along with the comfort and support of presence.

This vision of power raises an important warning: the powerless are so because the powerful do not recognize their own needs and place. Powerlessness is caused by the arrogance and condescension of the powerful.

THEOLOGY OF POWER

Theologians have tended to say little about God's power. Most systematic theology texts state, with little explication, that God is all-powerful, emphasizing God's unlimited authority and might, portraying God as a conqueror and victor. Mennonite theologian, J. C. Wenger, defined the omnipotent God as "able without limit to accomplish all divine purposes" (1954, p. 52). Jesus himself said, "All power in heaven and on earth has been given to me..." (Mt. 28:18).

But what can we mean when we affirm that God is all-powerful, omnipotent? Anna Case-Winters (1988) notes that the issue is not how *much* power God has, but *what kind* of power God has. As Gayle noted today, Case-Winters has encouraged a fundamental reconstruction of our understanding of divine omnipotence.

We do know a little. God is reliably powerful, peaceful and just, and resists evil. God has loving, compassionate power which liberates from bondage. God's determination to love and be merciful stands in tension with God's willingness to allow human autonomy. God chooses to draw near and engage in a dynamically loving relationship, allowing humans to affect the divine will. God will not dominate those with whom God wishes relationship.

Ours is a theology of unequal power since divine and human powers are unequal. Wenger stated, "God is the absolute sovereign, while humans are completely dependent creature" (1954, p. 54). However, this does not sound like Paul, who was not embarrassed to say, "I can do all things through Christ, who strengthens me" (Ph. 4:13). What can we mean, then, when we talk about God-given human power?

ETHICS OF POWER*

Each of us has power, has been robbed of power, has used power to harm another person or our community. Each of us must acknowledge that we have the potential to be victim, abuser, or therapeutic neighbor. Power is inherently neither right nor wrong: it is ambiguous. Power has great positive potential to enhance relationships, becoming an impetus for health when used rightly. But it also has great negative potential for distorting relationships.

Our theology of power must inform our ethics of power, value and voice. We know that ethics for the relatively powerless cannot be the same as for the powerful. The powerful must listen, must learn to hear those who know. It is the responsibility of the powerful to knowledgeably choose appropriate uses of power informed by the gospel of peace.

The only "right" use of power is turned in the service of others. Power is "wrong" in several instances. It is wrong to use power simply to demonstrate that I have it. Power is wrong if I am ignorant of it and I use my power unknowingly. In either instance, I become careless about vulnerability, denying my own need and vulnerability, and that of others. To know one's own power and to commit oneself to empowering others are necessary, but not sufficient conditions for preventing corruption and abuse of power.

---

*I acknowledge the insight of my friend, John Regehr, in formulating this section.

HEALING POWER: IMPLICATIONS FOR RESISTANCE

A relationship is a power-ful relationship: that is, each participant has power to effect powerful changes. As we can imagine, however, different understandings of power will effect the ways in which a relationship is managed to resist evil and create justice. How may we define "help" in the context of this discussion of power?

1. The dominating power model emphasizes the necessity of "strength" and entails the loss of personhood for the one being overpowered. The powerful in an ecclesial, familial or professional setting therefore lends the power of expertise or position to the powerless by allying against evil. Often the powerful will advocate for, even speak for and give voice to, the powerless.

2. The ability model acknowledges that diminishment and restriction of power is the source of pain and suffering. The powerful, here, give friendship which declares, "I will believe in you, value you. I will speak to you and help you to reflect, discover and refine your own agenda. You will accomplish."

3. The empowerment model recognizes that suffering can be voluntary, and that one can accept or even choose suffering for the good of another. The powerful resist evil, in effect, by saying, "I will support you, help you satisfy your needs, I will help you remove the barriers which hinder your growth. This will free you to develop and fulfill your potential."

Note that all three describe "help" which comes from unequal power--the powerful offers help to the powerless, often taking over the situation for the disempowered.

4. The solidarity model understands human vulnerability and acknowledges that the pain of one person harms all of us. This type of standing-with power resists evil on behalf of all humanity, transforming suffering and transcending individual pain by mutual alliance. It also acknowledges the wounds, caused by violence, of victim, abuser, family and community. Liberation is found, therefore, in solidarity. "I am with you in your pain. I will not leave you, we will comfort each other in our woundedness."

CONCLUSION

Again, thank you Gayle, for your thinking and pushing us about pacifist resistance. Behind what you have said has lurked ideas and questions about relationships and the impact of power. We must all choose to use our power creatively, to join with others in the struggle against violence, to build new relationships in which violence is obsolete.

REFERENCES

Case-Winters, Anna. "The Problem of Omnipotence: The Meaning of Power." *American Academy of Religion*, November 20, 1988.

Goodrich, Thelma Jean. "Women, Power and Family Therapy: What's Wrong with This Picture?" *Women and Power*, Thelma Jean Goodrich (Ed.). New York: W. W. Norton, 1991, chapter 1.

Wenger, John C. *Introduction to Theology*. Scottdale, Pa.: Herald Press, 1954.

Chapter 3

DOMESTIC ABUSE: A CASE STUDY

Isaac I. Block

Behind this study is a pastoral concern for the safety and wellbeing of all people in the family context. This means that the human situation rather than theological systems is the starting point. In pastoral theology, theology not only speaks to the human situation, but theological questions arise out of the human situation. Theology done this way may not have ready answers to all human dilemmas, but it affirms the legitimacy of the voices that raise the questions, and it gives hope to those asking the questions.

Having said this, I note the following theological presuppositions behind my work. First, for God, the act of creation was an act of empowering. Second, for Jesus, the act of dying was an act of laying aside power that belonged to him. Third, to strip people of their power through malicious conduct is a violation of the image of God implanted within them. It is an act of violence against God, for people are the image of God. Fourth, the creation order established the equality, though not the sameness, of females and males. It does not justify a hierarchy of any kind. Fifth, the fall into sin had the effect of disrupting the original order, but the principal of equality was not cancelled. The rule of the man over the woman belongs to the curse rather than to the creation order. Consequently it is not a positive reference point for succeeding generations. Sixth, the Christ event redeemed people from the curse. Oppressive structures and systems belong to the spiritual powers and principalities that must be resisted and overcome (Eph. 6). It is not by chance that the reference to dark spiritual powers and principalities follows the discussion of ordered human relationships in Ephesians 5. Seventh, followers of Jesus adopt a nonviolent life style. They build rather than break down. They do not seek positions of power, but empty themselves of what power they have for the benefit of those who are less powerful.

RATIONALE FOR THE STUDY

North American Mennonites, particularly through the work of the Mennonite Central Committee, are seen as people who live and work in a broken world "in the name of Christ." But what happens behind the closed doors of their homes? How do husbands and wives treat each other and their children? How were they treated by their parents? Is there domestic violence among Mennonites? The following report of a study in Winnipeg is an attempt to begin to answer these questions. The study was done between the fall of 1988 and the spring of 1991.

Through conducting a survey, I attempted to measure the quality of family relationships in one small professing Christian segment of society. The survey was intended to describe, not an ancient ideal, but a current reality. What follows is a report of this survey and its findings.

The study is based on two hypotheses. One is that there is abuse among Mennonites in Winnipeg. The other is that Mennonites in Winnipeg in abusive situations are turning to their pastors and/or the church for assistance. This hypothesis assumes a general pattern rather than exceptional cases.

In Manitoba there is some confusion over who the Mennonites are. Are they an ethnic group, or are they a religious group? Who is a real Mennonite? In this study the term Mennonite has a religious designation. It is used consistently with reference to people who are associated with a Mennonite congregation inside the perimeter of the City of Winnipeg. Also in this study, association with the church is determined by the inclusion of the persons' home telephone number in a Mennonite congregation's telephone directory.

The assumption is made that some persons will refuse to cooperate in this study for fear that their participation in it will exasperate their abusers. Consequently the frequency and severity of domestic abuse among Mennonites in Winnipeg probably exceeds the findings of this study.

A random sample was created for this study. It included telephone numbers from the directories of thirty-six Mennonite churches in Winnipeg. TABLE 1 shows the pattern of initial telephone responses.

TABLE 1
Initial Telephone Contacts

	NO ANSWER	FEMALE	MALE	TOTAL
PHONE CALLS	74	291	135	500
COOPERATE	0	173	80	253
RETURNED	1	132	54	187
NOT RETURNED	0	41	26	67

While none of the respondents who chose not to cooperate in the study were asked for an explanation, 17 volunteered the reason for declining in terms of an inability. The most frequent inability had to do with language limitations. Of these seventeen, sixteen were female while only one was male. Based on inability (largely due to language) 5.5% of the female respondents compared with .75% of the male respondents declined the invitation to cooperate.

A REPORT ON THE RETURNS

With regard to their readiness to cooperate, 59.39% of persons answering the telephone agreed to cooperate. The difference between males and females was .20% in favor of the females. But 76.3% of the females actually returned their questionnaires while only 67.5% of the males returned theirs.

The total number used in reporting the analysis is 187, the number of returned questionnaires. Percentages given are based on that number unless there is a specific reference to a different number.

The data indicate that on average, 2.84 people live in one household. This represents a total of 14,550 people (adults and children) in Winnipeg who are associated with a Mennonite church included in the study. The random sample of persons who returned their questionnaire was 1.29% of the total population.

If the original pool of 500 telephone numbers is used, 37.4% of the random sample returned their questionnaires. If the number of those answering the telephone is used (i.e. 426), 43.9% of the random sample returned the questionnaire. If the number of persons who agreed to cooperate is used (i.e. 253), 73.91% returned the questionnaire.

DEMOGRAPHICS

A general overview of the demographics is given below. Unless indicated otherwise, the information given is in percentages of the total number of respondents. Some of the percentages are shown to the nearest whole number.

Seventy-one percent of the respondents to the questionnaire were female, 29% were male. One respondent did not indicate the gender.

The following graph shows the number of people in the homes of the respondents.

Figure 1

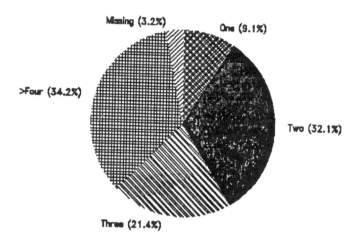

RANDOM SAMPLE POPULATION
People at Home

Missing (3.2%)   One (9.1%)

>Four (34.2%)

Two (32.1%)

Three (21.4%)

From the data it seems that in all probability these homes, for the most part, represent traditional households with a married couple having one or two children. The statistical mean per household is 2.834 people. The data on marital status indicate that 72% of the respondents were married, 20% were single, 5% were widowed, 1% were either divorced or separated, and 2% declined answering. Only 1.6% of the respondents were in a second marriage relationship.

Thirty-eight percent of the respondents indicated that there are one or more individuals under the age of 18 years living in their households.

The intent of this study is to focus on a religious group. Two factors address the issue of religion. First, all of the respondents are sufficiently close to the church to have their telephone numbers included in the church directories. Second, the questionnaire asks, "How often do you attend Sunday morning worship services each month?" The assumption here is that the more frequently the persons attend Sunday morning worship services, the more religious they are. The survey yielded the results displayed on the graph below.

Figure 2

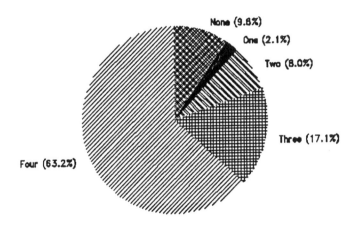

RANDOM SAMPLE POPULATION
Monthly Worship Practice

None (9.6%)
One (2.1%)
Two (8.0%)
Three (17.1%)
Four (63.2%)

On a scale of 1 to 4, (the number of Sunday morning worship services attended each month) the mean for the entire population surveyed is 3.562. Judging by this factor alone, the group surveyed is a highly committed religious group. In this sample group, there is no significant difference in the frequency of abuse based on worship attendance.

Eighty-five percent of the respondents reported that one or both of their parents were Mennonites.

Respondents were asked how long they had been married or living together. The graph below shows this data. It indicates a good cross-section of the population.

Figure 3

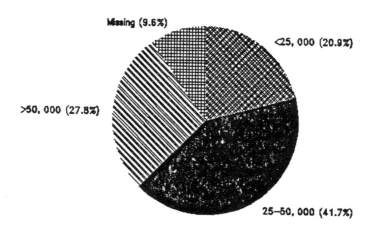

RANDOM SAMPLE POPULATION
Annual Income

Missing (9.6%)

<25, 000 (20.9%)

>50, 000 (27.8%)

25-50, 000 (41.7%)

Respondents were asked, "Have you had a marital relation-ship with another partner?" Only 1.6% said "Yes." They were also asked if their spouse had a marital relationship with another partner. Here 3.2% said "Yes."

The question, "How did the relationship end?" follows the question, "Have you had a marital relationship with another part-ner?" When asked how their relationships ended, .5% said through separation; 1.6% through divorce; 2.7% through death; and 1.1% responded under the category "OTHER". These data do not cor-respond exactly with the earlier data in which respondents declared their marital status.

An attempt was made to determine the level of education between the marriage partners. On a scale of 2 - 12 in which each number signified a level or particular kind of education, the mean for the respondents is 7.062 while the mean for the partner is 6.856. There is not a great disparity. On the scale, the number 6 indicates graduation from a Bible School or Bible College and the number 7 indicates some education at a community college. None of the respondents report they have no formal education.

There is a weak correlation between between the level of education of respondents and physical abuse, emotional abuse, and the destruction of pets and property. In each instance, the mean is highest for people who have achieved a Bachelor's level of education.

When asked in how many towns or cities they had lived during their married life, 47% of the total respondents reported they had lived in only one. This would have to be the City of Winnipeg. This indicates a relatively stable population. There is a weak correlation between the number of towns in which people have lived and the frequency of physical and emotional abuse and the destruction of pets and property. In each instance the mean is highest for people who have lived in two towns or cities.

Respondents were asked to estimate the total yearly family income. Three possibilities were given: under $25,000; between $25,000 and $50,000; and over $50,000. The graph below shows the results. The average was to the right of center. Yearly income has not significance in the frequency of abuse.

Respondents were asked to indicate their age. The findings can be shown as follows.

Figure 4

RANDOM SAMPLE POPULATION
Age

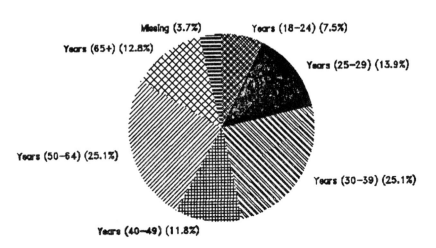

Respondents were asked to indicate their country of origin. Seventy-one percent reported that Canada was their country of origin. Eleven percent were from Eastern Europe. The rest were in small numbers from a variety of other countries.

A REPORT ON THE FINDINGS

This part of the report is organized around a series of sub-problems. Throughout this report, wherever there is a reference to totals, the number represents the lowest possible number. Some of the numbers on the questionnaire represent ranges of numbers. The actual totals could be significantly higher than those shown in this report.

Subproblem #1: Physical Abuse

What is the nature and frequency of physical abuse among persons associated with Mennonite churches in Winnipeg? Respondents were asked for two sets of data. First, they were asked to recall their growing up years and give the number of times their parents or guardians resorted to abusive behaviors in response to disputes in the family. Second, they were asked to give the number of times their partners had physically abused them in the last twelve months. The questionnaire does not define physical abuse. It asks about a variety of physical behaviors. Respondents had to determine if the behavior was abusive or if it was corrective. Table 2 below represents the numbers based on the lowest numbers of the various ranges in the questionnaire.

TABLE 2
Physical Abuse

	Childhood	Last Year
Threw Something	185	38
Pushed	290	13
Slapped	373	6
Threw at Someone	108	5
Hit with an Object	193	2
Beat Up	51	1
Kicked	94	0
Used Knife/gun	1	0
TOTALS	1,295	65

On the surface it appears as though the childhood years were much more violent than the last year, which represents a year as an adult. If, however, the childhood years are divided by the 18 years they represent, the total number of incidents per year is a fraction under 72.

When the frequency of abuse is presented in percentages, another interesting picture surfaces. The numbers shown are the percentages of the total populations that were surveyed. The College Population[1] was asked only about the last twelve months. The people in the random sample population were asked about their growing up years and about the last twelve months.

TABLE 3
Physical Abuse (Percentages)

	College Population	Random Population	
		Childhood	Last Year
Threw Something	29.2	15.1	5.4
Pushed	27.8	20.8	4.2
Slapped	15.0	20.8	2.2
Threw at Someone	18.1	11.2	1.6
Hit with an Object	8.4	14.9	1.1
Kicked	9.8	5.9	0
Beat Up	2.8	3.7	0.5
Used Knife/gun	0	0.5	0

The College population recalled approximately the same time period as respondents in the random sample who reported on the past twelve months. The frequency remembered by the College population is much higher than that of the random sample population. Indeed, it represents a high incidence of physical abuse. The difference between the two populations requires further study.

These data demonstrate that there is physical abuse among Menonites in Winnipeg. In varying numbers, each kind of abuse referred to in this section of the questionnaire is reported. In the random sample group there is no significance between physical abuse and gender.

Subproblem #2: Emotional Abuse
What is the nature and frequency of emotional abuse among persons associated with Mennonite churches in Winnipeg?

Again, respondents were asked for two sets of data. First,

they were asked to recall their growing up years and give the number
of times their parents or guardians resorted to emotionally abusive
behavior in response to disputes in the family. Second, they were
asked to give the number of times their partners emotionally abused
them in the last twelve months. The questionnaire does not define
emotional abuse. It asks about a variety of behaviors that could have
an emotional impact on someone. Respondents had to determine if
the behavior was abusive. The table below represents the numbers
based on the lowest numbers of the various ranges in the questionnaire.

TABLE 4
Emotional Abuse

	Childhood	Last Year
Sulked	72	69
Spited	50	38
Stomped out	56	36
Insulted	40	32
Got third party advice	27	9
Threatened to hit	36	5
Threatened with knife/gun	3	0
TOTALS	289	189

Once again, on the surface it appears that the abuse was more
frequent and more severe during the childhood years. However, if
children's limited ability to recall early childhood experiences is
taken into account, and if the childhood experiences are divided by
18 to arrive at an annual figure, the picture changes. The average
for childhood experiences is approximately 16 incidents per year for
the entire population as compared with 189 for the same population
in the last year.

The frequency of emotional abuse appears to increase
markedly in adulthood. Emotional abuse is more sophisticated than
physical abuse. This observation raises the possibility that Mennonites have taken seriously their doctrine of nonviolence. In practice though, they have tended to apply this to physical rather than
emotional violence.

It is important to see the data when translated into percentages of the total populations victimized by emotional abuse. The
College population reported only on the incidents of the past twelve

months while the people in the random sample reported on their growing up years and the last twelve months.

TABLE 5
Emotional Abuse (Percentages)

	College Population	Random Population Childhood	Last Year
Sulked	75.3	38.5	41.2
Spited	45.9	26.6	20.7
Stomped out	50.0	30.0	19.2
Insulted someone	41.6	21.4	15.6
Got third party advice	29.2	14.4	4.7
Threatened to hit	22.1	19.2	2.6
Threatened with knife/gun	0.0	1.6	0.0

These data demonstrate that there is emotional abuse among Menonites in Winnipeg. In varying numbers, each kind of abuse referred to in this section of the questionnaire is reported. Once again, in this sample group there is no significance between emotional abuse and gender.

Subproblem #3: Sexual Abuse

What is the frequency and nature of sexual abuse among persons associated with Mennonite churches in Winnipeg?

To arrive at this information, respondents were asked a series of questions. First, they were asked, "Were you ever the victim of a sexual violation" or an attempted sexual violation? Second, they were given nine options from which to indicate the kind of sexual abuse they had experienced. Two sets of data are available. The one set is gathered from the student population while the other is gathered from the random sample population. The percentages represent the number of persons in the sample who were sexually abused.

TABLE 6
Sexual Abuse (Percentage)

		College Sample	Random Sample
Ever Abused	(N=72) 19.4	(N=187)	19.8
Fondling of Breasts		4.2	7.0
Fondling of Genitals		2.8	7.0
Propositioning		1.4	5.3
Flirting		4.2	4.8
Inappropriate Holding		1.4	4.3
Forced Sex		8.3	3.7
Inappropriate Kissing		1.4	2.1
Other		1.4	1.1
Oral Sex		2.8	0.0

The numbers in the table represent the percentages of the total number of respondents in the two groups. The total number of student responses was 72 while the total number of responses in the random sample was 187. Judging by the first entry in the table, almost all people who will be sexually abused have been abused by the time they are through college. After that the kind of abuse varies, but it appears to remain within the original group.

Respondents were asked how often this happened to them in the past twelve months. One college student said twice and nine said once. In the random sample, one respondent said four and two said twice. If the sizes of the two populations are taken into account, it is clear that College students are much more open to sexual abuse than the people in the random sample.

In the student population, 27% of the female population reported they had been sexually violated. This figure must be compared with 25% of the females in the random sample population who reported having been sexually violated. In the student male population, 15% reported they had been sexually violated while in the random sample male population only 7% reported they had been violated. It follows from this that females continue to be vulnerable in adulthood while males become less vulnerable in adulthood. In the student population 1.4% reported they had been violated in the past year. In the random sample 3.2% reported they had been violated in the past year. Judging by these data, the pool of people being abused continues to increase after adulthood. This finding is inconsistent with the information in response to the question, "Were

you ever the victim of a sexual violation?" The response for both
population groups was the same, slightly under 20% of the total populations that were surveyed.

An examination of the factors that ask who the abusers were
yields some interesting data. The numbers given are the percentages
of the two total populations. The numbers in brackets indicate the
actual number of persons who reported this abuse.

TABLE 7

Identity of Sexual Abuser

	College Population		Random Population	
STRANGER	(2)	2.8	(13)	7.0
OTHER	0		(11)	5.9
BROTHER	(2)	2.8	(9)	4.8
FRIEND	(6)	8.3	(6)	3.2
RELATIVE	(2)	2.8	(6)	3.2
FATHER	(1)	1.4		0
MOTHER		0		0
SISTER		0		0
GRANDFATHER		0		0
GRANDMOTHER		0		0

Not all sexual abuse experienced by respondents was
domestic abuse. Respondents reported having been abused by
strangers, friends, and child care givers. In the college population,
friends are the most frequent abusers. The questionnaire did not ask
for an explanation. At least this much must be said of the college
population, friends violate friends.

As shown in TABLE 7, in the population of the random
sample, strangers are the most frequent abusers. The category of
"other" is nondescript. The frequency with which brothers, relatives,
and friends are abusers is disappointing. If it is true that brothers,
relatives, and friends are trusted people, then, if these groups are
placed into one category of trusted people, these people represent
the most frequent sexual violators.

These data demonstrate that there is sexual abuse among
Mennonites in Winnipeg. In varying numbers, each kind of abuse
referred to in this section of the questionnaire is reported. Here
there is significant correlation between sexual abuse and gender. In
this sample group, women are more vulnerable than men.

Subproblem #4: Destruction of Pets and Properties

What is the nature and frequency of malicious attacks on favorite pets and properties? The forms of malicious attacks were selling and/or destroying a partner's favorite pets or properties. The information below gives the percentages of the total populations surveyed who experienced this abuse. The numbers in brackets indicate the number of incidents. The College population reported only on the experiences of the last twelve months.

TABLE 8
Destruction of Pets and Property

	College Population	Random Population Childhood	Last Year
Destroyed Favorite Property	(3) 4.2	(25) 3.6	(4) 1.0
Sold Favorite Property	(3) 4.2	(24) 2.1	(21) 1.0
Destroyed Favorite Pet	(2) 2.8	(22) 1.6	(3) 0.5
Sold Favorite Pet	0	(1) .5	0

The two columns that offer possibilities for comparison are the College population and the last year of the random population. The College population is more likely to be victimized in this manner than the random population.

These data demonstrate that there is abuse among Mennonites in Winnipeg that takes the form of destroying favorite pets and properties. In varying numbers, each kind of abuse referred to in this section of the questionnaire is reported. There is no significance between the frequency of this form of abuse and gender.

Subproblem #5: Resources for Victims

Where do abused persons associated with Mennonite churches in Winnipeg go for help?

Respondents in both the College population and the random population were asked where they turn for help when they are abused. In TABLE 9, "General" refers to all forms of reported abuse other than sexual. Again the numbers are percentages of the total populations surveyed.

TABLE 9
Support Resources for Victims of Abuse

	College Population General Sexual		Random Population General Sexual	
Family Member	47.2	6.9	2.7	7
Friend	47.2	8.3	5.3	5.9
Minister	8.3	1.4	2.1	1.1
Other	1.4		0.5	1.1
Social Worker	4.2		0.5	0.5
Marriage Counsellor	1.4		1.1	0.5
Lawyer			0.5	
Church Member	9.7	1.4	1.6	
Psychologist	2.8	1.4	0.5	
Medical Doctor			2.1	
Counsellor			1.6	
Legal Aid			1.1	
Child Care			1.1	
Court			0.5	
Shelter			0.5	
Police				
Shelter Counsellor				

For purposes of this report, the most important data are those that comment on the extent to which people in abusive situations turn to the church for help. Notwithstanding the data from a recent survey of Winnipeg Mennonite pastors,[2] only a small number of people who have been sexually violated go to the pastors or to church members for help. In both population groups of sexually abused persons, friends and family members are the persons most frequently sought out for help. For other forms of abuse, significantly more victims from the college population go to their pastors or to other members of the church. They also seek out friends and family members in large numbers.

Although 95% of the pastors surveyed would counsel victims of abuse to see their medical doctors, in practice, only 2.1% of the random population visited their physicians on account of the abuse. None of these visits were prompted by their having been sexually abused.

It seems from the data that both populations were reluctant to seek professional help of any kind. The reason for this is not clear from the data. This is a matter that requires further inquiry.

Subproblem #6: Level of Satisfaction

How satisfied were respondents with the help they received
from the minister and/or church member? Respondents were asked
to indicate the level of their satisfaction at two places in the survey:
after reporting on their experiences of the past twelve months, and
after reporting on their experiences of sexual abuse. The following
table gives the data in percentages of the total populations surveyed.
It should be noted that in both samples, large numbers of respondents did not answer the question.

TABLE 10
Level of Satisfaction With Help Received

| | College Population | | Random Population | |
	General	Sexual	General	Sexual
Very Satisfied	16.7	1.4	4.3	6.4
Somewhat Satisfied	29.2	4.2	3.2	2.1
Mixed Experiences	5.6	2.8		1.1
Somewhat Dissatisfied	4.2	1.4		
Very Dissatisfied			.5	.5
Not Sure	8.3	2.8		

While about 46% of the College population were somewhat
satisfied or very satisfied with the help they received regarding "general" (i.e. other than sexual) abuse, only 5.6% were either somewhat
satisfied or very satisfied with the help they received regarding sexual
abuse. The number of people from both populations that went to
either the pastor or a church member is too small to establish the
level of satisfaction with the help received from these two sources.
Only general observations can be made. The College population
tended to be satisfied with the help they received for abuse that was
other than sexual. This population is ambivalent about the help
received to deal with their sexual abuse. In light of the fact that
friends and family members were the most frequent helpers, a case
could be made to advise college students to seek professional help
for their sexual abuse.
    The population in the random sample is more positive about
the help received. This may be at least in part because they are

generally more resourceful in seeking help and because they depend less on the informal help of friends and family members.

While small numbers of victims of abuse go to their pastors or the church for counsel, the survey of the random sample does not support the hypothesis that persons in abusive situations are turning to them for help. There is some movement in that direction by the College population in areas of nonsexual abuse. The fact that over 47% of College students turn to their friends and over 47% of them turn to their families makes it possible for families and friends to report to pastors. If this is the case, then it follows that the present primary role of the pastors is to support family and friends who are trying to help victims. This is a significant pastoral role, but it does not deal directly with the victims.

CONCLUSION

Based on this study, the hypothesis that there is evidence of domestic abuse among Mennonites in Winnipeg can be sustained. At the same time, however, the hypothesis that Mennonites in Winnipeg are turning to their pastors for assistance cannot be sustained on the basis of the same studies. That pastors are dealing with the issue of abuse is clear. What is less clear is who the people are that come to the pastors with reports of abuse. That is an issue that requires further investigation.

Based on this study it is not possible to make comparative comments with other religious or non-religious groups. To do this, further studies with similar methodologies and survey instruments would have to be used.

The findings and claims of this study must remain somewhat tentative until they are validated by a second study. In the meantime, however, the findings are sufficiently clear to indicate that the Mennonite churches of Winnipeg are not immune to the problem of abuse. While they put forth a concerted effort to provide services for disadvantaged communities and people around the world, they must also turn inward and put considerably more effort into dealing with the issue of abuse within their congregations.

NOTES

1. In a separate survey, seventy-two students at two Mennonite Bible Colleges in Winnipeg completed an abbreviated questionnaire.

2. Isaac I. Block, "Response to Domestic Abuse," *Journal of Mennonite Studies*, Summer, 1990, 190, 191. In the summer of 1989 the writer interviewed 41 senior pastors of Mennonite churches in Winnipeg. This included all of the pastors for whom a telephone listing was available. The 41 pastors who were surveyed reported having heard a total of well over one thousand reports of abuse in the last twelve months. These included at least 45 reports of sexual abuse, about 350 reports of physical abuse, about 600 reports of emotional abuse, about 90 reports of malicious treatment of pets and property, plus a smaller number under the category of "Other."

RESPONSE

Carolyn Holderread Heggen

Thank you, Isaac, for the passion and sustained energy you have put into planning and designing this research, into carrying it out and now into sharing your results with us here. I appreciate the pastoral concern which underlies this project and salute you for your sensitivity to the human situation out of which this research grows. I hope this work has whetted your interest in doing further research on this important topic. In our efforts to stop abuse against the vulnerable among us it is critical to have data with which we can better understand the problems we face.

Without having seen you research instrument or a description of your statistical design and analysis, it is not possible for me to comment on the statistical validity of your findings and conclusions. I assume someone with access to these has given you guidance and feedback. The raw data you report in your presentation does verify what many others have observed clinically, pastorally and personally: some Mennonites do commit abusive acts against family members.

You stated in your presentation that theological questions arise out of the human experience of abuse. I surely agree with you. I also contend, based upon my own work, that theological assumptions feed into the experience of abuse. While it has not been proven that certain religious beliefs *cause* abuse, clinicians have observed that some beliefs appear to interact with other factors to provide an environment where abuse can occur, where would-be abusers find it possible to justify their behavior through a distortion or extension of religious teachings, and where victims find it hard to stop the abuse. I would challenge Isaac and other researchers among us to move beyond the documentation of abuse (important as that surely is) to determining the theological assumptions and religious beliefs of both abusing and abused Mennonites.

Most of my research has not focused exclusively on a Mennonite population, although it has included Mennonite respondents. The general questions with which I have been working are: "What is the relationship between religious beliefs and mental health?" or "How do certain religious beliefs impact psychological health?" and specifically, "How do certain religious beliefs affect women's self-esteem and sense of personal empowerment?" I believe that to get to the bottom of the problem of abuse among our people we must better understand this relationship.

My doctoral research[1] looked at the internalization in Christian women of the belief that because of creation ordinance and divine plan for interpersonal human relationships, women should live in submission to men in the home and in the church. A strong correlation was found between this belief and lower levels of self-esteem. The more strongly a woman believed that because of her gender she should submit to male authority, the lower her level of self-esteem.

So what? What does this have to do with the topic of this consultation? Researchers have identified a strong link between low self-esteem and characteristics which are related to being able to protect oneself and one's children from an abusive person. People with low self-esteem feel isolated, unable to defend themselves, disempowered, and afraid of confronting or angering others.

In her book *Toward a New Psychology of Women,* Jean Baker Miller[2] discusses the psychological effects of internalizing a domination/subordination model of interpersonal relationships. She observes that a primary difficulty for both the person who dominates and the person who is subordinate is conceiving the subordinated person as of as much intrinsic worth as the dominating person. Miller also notes that people in subordinate positions are encouraged to develop personal psychological characteristics which are pleasing to the dominant people. These traits include submissiveness, passivity, docility, dependency, lack of initiative and the inability to act or think decisively. These are qualities which seem more characteristic of children than of a healthy adult. And perhaps more importantly, these qualities which may make it hard for a woman to protect herself and her children against an abusive mate.

Subordinates must adopt these characteristics to be considered well-adjusted. The Christian woman is encouraged to develop these qualities, not just to be considered well-adjusted, but also to be considered godly. One day a client came into my office and cried, "I feel I can't be a good Christian woman and an emotionally healthy person at the same time." As she talked further she told of having been raised in an abusive, alcoholic home. Not surprisingly, she had grown up, left home and married an abusive, alcoholic man. Subsequently she experienced spiritual conversion and joined a dynamic evangelical church. Close to the same time she joined a group for adult children of alcoholics where she was told she needed to stop feeling so responsible for everyone's well-being, she needed to face and feel her anger, she needed to stop doing anything and everything to keep peace, she needed to stop being so passive and submissive to her abusive husband, and she needed to stop forgiving him so quickly and easily. The dilemma for her was that she felt this would put her in violation of what her church taught about being a good Christian wife.

The perceived conflict for this client in seeking psychological healing and being a good Christian wife led me to study clergy's beliefs and teachings to women about godly behavior and spirituality. A colleague and I asked pastors and priests to describe spiritually healthy men, women and adults of unspecified gender. We found that clergy tend to describe spiritually healthy women as being markedly different from spiritually healthy men. They described spiritually healthy women as, among other things, "obedient and yielding," "submissive," "defers to others for advice," "willing to have spouse make decisions," "reluctant to criticize the behavior of others," and "finds identity through others." (These findings are reported in the April, 1988 issue of *Counseling and Values*.) If a woman embodies these characteristics which are considered important to be a spiritual, godly woman, she may find it hard to confront abusive behavior directed toward her and her children. If her children experience her as a submissive, powerless person, they are less likely to go to her for help when they are victimized by someone else.

Let's not fool ourselves; it *does* matter what people believe. There is a relationship between abuse and theology. Isaac's research and the countless stories of victimization which are coming out of our churches and families tell us that we have a serious abuse problem among us. I would hope that this weekend will be the beginning of ongoing work which will help us understand how some of our teachings have affected human relationships and are related to abuse and poor emotional health. I trust this will be a time when we can together discover alternative ways of interpreting some biblical passages, ways which will be both faithful to the intent of the Spirit and Good News for women, men and children.

I'm delighted that you here in this theological enclave have invited us from the psychological community, those of us who work in the trenches, to dialogue with you. For too long our disciplines have been seen as oppositional. The issue of theology and abuse is too important and too complex not to be given our best combined insights and efforts. I think this consultation is an important step in that direction.

NOTES

1. "Dominance/Submission Role Beliefs, Self Esteem and Self Acceptance in Christian Lay Women." Unpublished dissertation, University of New Mexico, 1989.

2. Boston: Beacon Press, 1976. See especially chapter 1.

CHRISTIAN IDEOLOGY, RAPE AND WOMEN'S POSTRAPE JOURNEYS TO HEALING*

Ruth E. Krall

As a pastoral theologian, I am concerned with clinical and spiritual epistemologies. Our various academic disciplines shape our ways of knowing and our methodologies for gathering data. In a cross-disciplinary consultation, it is necessary to clarify the parameters within which we create knowledge and theories. Because of my interdisciplinary interests, I am going to make some assumptions here which I probably should now clarify.

1. Healing is not the same as curing. Healing begins within the person who seeks wholeness. Healing is not something done to the person by others. Healing involves the whole bodySelf,[1] its cognitive beliefs and values, and its social networks of relationality. When wholeness is shattered for an individual, each of these domains experiences the shattering. By necessity then, the search for healing involves the bodySelf, its cognitive patterns of organizing ideation, and networks of social relationality. In the complexities of wholeness and brokenness, the shattering of wholeness is akin to death and loss; the creation of a new wholeness is akin to birth and resurrection. The times of shattering and the times of rebirthing, then, become times of great liminality. These are the times within an individual's life which present thresholds of great danger and great potential. In any liminal search for wholeness, the individual may create a more dysfunctional bodySelf or she may give birth to a strong, well-functioning bodySelf.

2. Cultural worldviews shape our descriptions of wholeness and our descriptions of brokenness. Deeply embedded within cultural processes, each individual early learns and internalizes the deepest myths of her or his own culture. Some of this learning is intuitive and preverbal and is, therefore, hidden from direct awareness. Some of this learning is encapsulated within specific language

---

*Based on a chapter in my book, tentatively titled *Rape's Power to Dismember Women's Lives*. (Cleveland, Ohio: Pilgrim Press, forthcoming).

or discourse patterns. These patterns of vocabulary, syntax, and grammar embody a particular culture's patterns of organizing the knowable and the forbidden. The cultural prejudices of language shape an individual's ability to learn and to know. These prejudices establish the parameters of personalized consciousness itself.

I think of internalized worldviews as a set of cultural blinders. Blinders, on a horse, establish the boundaries of direct knowing for the horse and create an artificial barrier to complete awareness. Cultural blinders, I believe, do the same for humans. In times of perceived well-being, the complex bodySelf does not ask questions of its relationships within culture. The inchoate questions which are implicit within worldviews remain obscure, vague, and indefinite. The bodySelf is unaware of its lack of awareness. However, in times of shattering, cultural blinders are often shattered as well. When the bodySelf shatters, the worldviews of the bodySelf also shatter. New awarenesses develop about culturally conditioned prejudices which were once implicit in the bodySelf's experiences of personal and relational wholeness.

3. Rape in a woman's life is such a shattering event. Her journey to healing involves bushwhacking a path through a distorted, surreal landscape in which nothing appears the same as it did before the rape. Once raped, the woman finds that her familiar bodySelf is no longer familiar to her. She encounters a strange bodySelf that is perversely similar to the one she knew, while simultaneously being totally unrecognizable. Once raped, the woman finds her comfortable worldview is no longer comfortable. Once raped, the woman knows that her secure relationships are not a guaranteed source of security. Once shattered by the experience of rape, the woman must journey into and through her awareness of rage-filled grief for the lost or destroyed bodySelf. I know a woman who, after rape, experienced terror at not finding her recognizable bodySelf. I can still hear the terrible anguish of her shrieks and cries. Her repeated insistence that "I want my old self back and I can't find her," reverberates still in my consciousness.

In addition to journeying into and through rage and grief, the post-rape woman must journey into and through the determined labors of birthing a new bodySelf. Sunday's (September 29, 1991) *South Bend Tribune* carried the story of a woman alone at work. In the midst of sudden pushing contractions, she delivered herself a breach-birth baby by reaching into her own vagina and pulling it out of her body. Having safely delivered her own baby, she rested on the floor until medical attendants arrived. This incredible story of a woman's courage in a time of great personal danger, can stand as a metaphor for the courage needed by postrape women who must re-create both themselves and their worlds. Out of their postrape awarenesses, they must courageously push and pull new bodySelves into life.

FEMINIST SCHOLARSHIP

Feminist scholarship has focused attention on several topics which relate to my concerns for postrape women. Theologians such as Carol Christ[2] and Nelle Morton[3] have guided us into the aware-ness that women's stories and women's experiences are essential to theological reflection. Clinicians such as Anne Wilson Schaef[4] and Judith Herman[5] teach us that women's experiences and stories must be included as we think about the healing disciplines and our work with women clients. In a similar manner, radical feminist theorists such as Andrea Dworkin[6] and Angela Davis[7] insist that the particu-larities of women's experience be acknowledge, recognized and vali-dated.

Women's experiences of rape, as part of the story of their individual lives, is a legitimate place to think about the intersection of theology with the clinical disciplines. Women's stories about their personal encounters with rape become the foundation upon which a more inclusive theology can be developed. To ask questions of theology from the perspectives of those women who have been vio-lated by rape, is to ask new questions of our theology or, perhaps more accurately, of our theologies.

The Story of Rape

The story of rape, then, is largely a girl's and women's story. Sometimes men and male children are raped. But in the United States and Canada today, rape is mostly done to females. Today's theological work, therefore, begins with the story of heterosexual rape. Last week's news carried the story of a ten year old boy who raped a 48 year old woman by holding her hostage with a gun. For the past year and a half I have been following a series of such stories about pre-adolescent male children who rape female children and women. Our culture's violence and preoccupation with sexual con-quest are now allowing immature boys the privileges once allowed only to fully grown men. Done by men and boys to women and girls, rape is experienced by women as violence and violation.

While men and women each have cultural stories about rape, each gender's specific stories present very different perspectives. Anthropologists who study rape in human cultures[8] describe rape not as an aberration of individual males, but rather as the permitted and sometimes encouraged patterns of gender relationality within patriarchal cultures. Patriarchal structures of knowing and doing objectify the woman as an inferior being who is expected to serve and obey the man. Subjugated to men's power over her and to masculine privilege in defining cultural standards of relationality, the woman is consistently disempowered by patriarchal assumptions and premises.

Living inside a patriarchal culture, the woman who is raped encounters her own psyche's embeddedness within the assumptions and values of patriarchy. The woman's life, from birth to death, is shaped by her relationships and by her own consciousness of those relationships. External relationships of male dominance and internal structures of feminine consciousness exist always in a dialogical relationship. Non-disrupted, unexamined female life within patriarchy accepts patriarchal premises as natural and normal. Patriarchy feels natural and secure. Women, just like men, accept their gender roles and socialization as their culture's normative ways of arranging life.

However, rape in a woman's life causes intense self-other examination. The patriarchal premises of her culture become more transparent. Once hidden from her awareness, she now sees--however vaguely and incompletely--the premises of her culture as the framework of her postrape suffering. That which she once accepted without question becomes that which she must now question with an intensity that often frightens her. I know a woman who survived a particularly brutal rape. Once her physical healing was assured, she began to examine each and every relationship for evidence of male dominance. That examination caused her to resign, eventually, from a job where her boss made sexual remarks to women employees as a form of male teasing. It led her, in subsequent job interviews, to insist upon equitable salary and benefit packages for her work. She said to me, "These small rapes in my life must stop if I am to heal myself from what that man did to me when he physically raped me. I can no longer tolerate being raped every day."

The postrape woman begins with the intuition that rape has forever changed her. Once this comprehension is recognized and accepted, she moves into an understanding that rape has changed her world of relationality as well. Slowly she comprehends that all her personalized structures of knowing, being, and doing must be examined. She begins the reconstruction of the bodySelf. She begins an intense search for culturally complicit factors in her postrape suffering. Her introspective discoveries lead her to journey into the structural stories of her culture about maleness and femaleness; in essence, she slowly finds her way to the study and analysis of her culture's beliefs about Creation. She begins, however incompletely, to understand that her culture's beliefs about maleness and femaleness, in a multiplicity of formulations and interpretations, are the matrix for sexual violence and for her postrape anguish. The rape of her body, which she most likely experienced in total isolation from protecting others, becomes recognized as a valued and protected story within her culture. She comes to understand that rape is profoundly social. Rape-prone cultures, such as that of the United States, *promote* the rape of women. Rape promotion is one way in which patriarchal values are protected and maintained.

The unholy cycle is complete. Rape-prone cultures promote rape; rape occurs within cultures that tolerate, accept, and promote rape. To protect an individual woman against rape, the culture's most basic myths must change. For the culture's myths to change, its theology must change. The West's story of creation must be re-examined. For a rape-prone culture to change into a rape-free culture, maleness and femaleness must become something other than what they now are. Violence against women is embedded within Western values of women's inferiority and their consequent servility to men.

Mary Daly, feminist philosopher and theologian, utilized anthropological research in her analysis of patriarchal patterns of social organization. She writes that patriarchy is "a society manufactured and controlled by males; a fatherland, a society in which every legitimated institution is entirely in the hands of males and a few selected henchwomen, a society characterized by oppression, repression, depression, narcissism, cruelty, racism, classism, ageism, etc."[9]

A serious discussion of rape in the West involves some necessary discussion of Christianity's patriarchal worldview. As an organizing principle of culture, patriarchy is envisioned by feminist scholars as the fundamental problem in rape. A patriarchal worldview is one which sees maleness as the norm for human societies, while femaleness is seen as the deviation from the norm. It is one in which men speak and women listen; one in which men command and women obey; one in which men are the masters and women are the servants. A patriarchal society is one in which sexual violence is permitted, taught, and encouraged among men. Patriarchal societies are those in which men are taught to claim power over others (children, women, and weaker men) as a birthright. In these societies women are taught to see themselves a men's belongings or property. Powerless to affect the realities which affect them, women, in patriarchal societies, are encouraged to think of themselves as powerless.

The patriarchal mandate is that women need to accept, unquestioningly, systems of male dominance over them. To enforce such a mandate, patriarchal systems create blinders and boundaries for knowing. Among women, it is common to hear language such as the following: "I feel contained. There is a glass ceiling or glass barrier. I cannot get outside of or around the barriers that surround my life." These words, and others like them, are the language signals that point towards women's domestication within patriarchal cultures.

I am aware that the above formulation is an uncomfortable one for many of us. Descriptions of patriarchy as Christendom's organizing pattern for maleness and femaleness are usually not allowed into our awareness. We resist hearing them. We resent hearing them. Such a naming, by and of itself alone, creates anger and rage. When we combine an analysis of patriarchal realities with descriptions of Christendom and rape, we have narrated a volatile story that can explode around us.

Rape stories have incredible power in the lives of men and women. The topic of rape divides men and women in ways that no other topic does. Men's rage appears to focus itself on women's analysis of male privilege and power. To describe patriarchy in such blunt terms appears to create hostility between the two genders. Some men may feel unjustly blamed for other men's rape of women.

Women's rage, on the other hand, is more specific. Women's rage is based in their awareness that they cannot protect themselves from rape in a rape-prone culture. Many times they have shielded men from gaining an awareness of their gender specific anger, rage, and terror. Knowing that men often explode in direct anger or simmer with indirect rage when their power or privilege is threatened, women intuitively know that a discussion of patriarchy and rape is dangerous to them. They protect themselves by hiding their rage and terror from men's eyes.

The issue of women's silence about rape and the shattering of that silence is an underlying concern of mine in the presentation today. The more I learn about the complicated relationship of event and interpretation of event, the more clear I become that our language is a critical issue as we construct meaning. The language which we use to define a problem, will be the language which we must then use to solve it. It is in and through the constraints of our language that we begin to understand reality.

It is questionable if any human can cognitively process any raw experience of life without the use of language. But the use of language, by its very embeddedness within a culture's worldview, shapes experience and transforms it into something which can be shared and known.

To begin to theologize out of women's and men's stories about rape, is, necessarily, to confront issues of male power and privilege. This confrontation leads inevitably, I believe, to a discussion of Christian beliefs about maleness and femaleness. Christianity has shaped Western values about the proper, or natural, or normative relationships of men and women. It is acceptance of patriarchy as the "right" way to organize these relationships, Christianity has fostered men's privilege and power. It has done so by denying women's full humanity. And, wittingly or unwittingly, Christian theology and Christian ideology have sanctioned a worldview that fosters and promotes men's violence against women.

PATRIARCHAL CHRISTIAN THEOLOGY

Very early in the Christian centuries, male theologians and biblical exegetes interpreted Scriptures in ways which pronounced a doctrine of feminine evil.[10] Woman, they taught, was the creature who beguiled Adam and brought human sin into the world. For example, Tertullian, a theologian from the early church (ca CE 160 - 230), taught that each woman was an Eve. As an Eve she destroyed God's image on earth, the man. He saw the human male as created in God's image while the human female was created, secondarily, in the image of the man. Created *from* the man, the woman was created *for* the man, and was intended by God to serve the man.

John Chrysostom (ca CE 345 - 407), patriarch of Constantinople, taught that women were white sepulchers filled with pus, phlegm, and all uncleanliness. Because of their filth as menstruating women, men were taught to regulate the woman, to mold and tame her. What was essential in the relationship of men to women was the woman's submission and obedience to the man.

Jerome (ca CE 340 - 420), one of the most influential theologians of the pre-medieval church and an early translator of Scripture, believed that Eve was responsible for Adam's sin and that she, therefore, was responsible for God's decision to drive Adam and Eve away from the garden of Eden. Seeing menstruation as a sign of God's curse, he believed that nothing was so unclean as a menstruating woman.

Augustine (ca CE 354 - 430), probably the most influential pre-medieval theologian, taught that woman is not made in God's image, for only the man is created in God's image. He believed that the man's fall into original sin was occasioned by the woman's temptation. The woman, therefore, is responsible for sin's presence in the world.

Gradually the church accepted a doctrine of maleness and femaleness which declared that God created Adam in God's image and Eve in Adam's image. The man carries a bit of God within, even though sin has occurred, while the woman's humanity carries only the man's image within. The man becomes the prototype of true humanity while the woman carries only the shadow of humanity. In her created state of weakness, the woman caused Adam to sin. Second in creation and first in sin, the woman was believed to be cursed by God with the man's domination over her.[11]

By the thirteenth century, Aquinas (CE 1225 - 1274) taught Christians that woman was the source of men's sexual arousal. Seeing her presence in situations where men experienced uncontrolled erections, Aquinas blamed women for causing men to lust. Believing that the woman was created by God only to assist humanity with reproduction, she now became for Aquinas, the source of man's original sin, that sin which caused men to be unable to control their sexual desires.

Inasmuch as procreation was the only acceptable reason for coitus to occur, the possibility for conception formed one basis for the medieval custom of ranking sexual sins. Masturbation and homosexuality became unnatural since conception could not occur. Therefore, they were ranked as much graver sins than incest or rape in which conception could occur. One consequence of this medieval ranking was that the church began to teach its people that incest and rape were less serious sins than masturbation and homosexuality.

In addition to its ranking of sexual sins, the medieval church fixated on the virgin as God's ideal woman. Three fairly depersonalized views of women's sexuality emerged: whore, virgin, or wife. In this paradigm, the whore came to represent women's depraved carnality--that sin of every Eve which continued to tempt men; the virgin came to represent spiritual maleness because she subdued her female nature and its bodily desires; the wife came to represent maternity and submission. Taught by the church to submit to her husband who "is her head," the woman became the man's property. Her husband gained property rights over the woman's body, her choices, and her possessions.[12]

In this medieval view, the woman's body and sexuality became signs of her sinful female nature. Both the church and secular rulers taught men and women that because of her sinfulness, she must be subdued by the man/men who control her. Fathers, spouses, sons, brothers, and religious men were all given control of the woman. Medieval church and government agreed: in order to contain the sexual pollution of her female nature, the woman must be made to submit and obey, even though this was not her personal inclination. Church and government taught that undomesticated women created havoc in men's lives by threatening their salvation. Only in women's willing submission to men's rule could men and women both find salvation.

By the twentieth century an additional set of understandings emerged within some Christian communities: a doctrine of women's suffering. Women who suffer in violent, abusive relationships are taught that they must share in Christ's sufferings on the cross. A willingness to suffer at the hands of husband, son, father, or other responsible male is seen as desirable. As women willingly suffer at men's hands, they share in Christ's redemptive work on earth. One part of some women's Christian walk, therefore, is to model their lives after Christ's salvific suffering and death. In quietness and unprotesting submission, they are to accept men's violence towards their bodySelves. In so doing they may rescue his soul.

In addition, some contemporary Christians teach women that the husband functions as God in the marital relationship and that the wife is to obey her husband as if he were her God. Inasmuch as men are made in the image of God and women are made in man's image, the man is seen as the natural head of the woman. Only as she enacts submissive obedience to the man who commands here is she faithful to God.

The West's patriarchal worldview, shaped in large part by Christian theology and ideology, has been adopted and adapted to fit a scientific era as well. Aquinas believed that the complete prototypical human was male, while the female was a misbegotten creature. The complete male human was believed to be present in each male sperm. Via intercourse, the embryonic male was implanted in the female uterus. The woman, in this model, served as an incubator. If a boy were born, the male seed had hatched properly; but if a girl were born, she was misbegotten. In this model the female is defined by the absent penis which establishes full humanity, and by her uterus which is her sole reason for being.

When the microscope was invented, the power of this belief was embedded in male scientists as well as in theologians. When scientists looked for the first time at male sperm in the microscopic field, they saw within the sperm the complete human male embryo in miniature. So powerful was the theological vision of Western culture that real humanness resides in maleness, that these scientists confirmed it as objective, verifiable data. The cultural belief that presupposed maleness as humanness determined the visual examination of the sperm.

Women's challenges to patriarchal understandings of maleness and femaleness yield many emotions in each one of us. As women challenge the prevailing cultural view that they are defined only by their sexuality, they are also creating space for other views of maleness and femaleness. If they are no longer the "second sex," and if they are more than incubators of the male seed, and if they are created in God's image, then the theological certainties of the West's Christian centuries are under siege. As women challenge the traditional and historical theological understandings of Christian ideology, they are free to ask new questions about their experiences. Ancient theological understandings have begun to give way to these new questions. The presence of the feminist woman, newly freed from patriarchal understandings of God and people, has begun to cause new theological moments to occur.

OBEDIENCE AND DISMEMBERMENT

It is my opinion that the issue of women's subordination to men, most specifically the cultural demand that women obey men, is one of two issues which must be dealt with in understanding the woman who has been raped. The second of these agendas is terror. Other than acknowledging terror as one major reality for women as they encounter a rapist in their lives, today's presentation will not deal further with this topic.

Vis à vis obedience, then, rape's authority to alter women's lives lies in rape's reminder to women that they are expected to obey men's commands without any question or challenges to his authority. Any operational definition of rape must include awareness of the rapist's power over the woman. Once a woman is in an inevitable rape situation, she encounters the rapist's claim for absolute power over her.

Perceiving herself as powerless to do more than attempt survival, the woman reacts to rape with her total bodySelf. She searches for her own route out of potentially lethal and always dangerous interpersonal transaction. Powerless to stop the rapist from his assault on her bodySelf, the woman enters into processes of compliance and submission. She does whatever she is commanded to do in the hope that she will not inadvertently trigger him into battering, mutilating or murdering her.

The single most important central dynamic of rape is the rapist's demand that the woman accept a powerless position in which she obeys his unilateral commands. Only he defines the field of their interaction. Only he establishes the rules for their relationship. No amount of prayer-like pleading from the woman will dissuade him from his self-appointed task of overpowering and subduing the woman. No amount of struggle will dissuade him from his work. Like the gods, he destroys without explanation.

It is sufficient for the rapist to know that he is in control of their shared history and that the woman is not. Establishing himself as an omnipotent ruler, upon whom she is totally dependent for survival and life, the rapist enacts his power through her weakness, through her obedience to him. In the rape event, he claims her body as if it belonged only to him.

Not only bound to the rapist by terror now, the woman is bound to him by his insistence upon her subjugation to his will. Miriam Simos[13] describes how patriarchal systems of authority colonize the minds of the powerless. Because patriarchal cultures condition the woman to obey masculine systems of authority, a direct encounter with any one of these systems (rape, for example) further acculturates the woman to future obedience. In these encounters there is always an explicit threat of something worse happening if there is disobedience. In addition, there is usually the promise of less harmful consequences with continuing obedience behaviors.

In situations of coercive violence, victims usually believe the person who is in control of the situation. Isolated from helpful others, they have no certain way of validating the victimizer's information. Thus it is that women in a rape situation believe their rapist's claims and comply with the rapist's rules. Believing that their survival is dependent upon compliance, they submit.

These compliance behaviors, even when absolutely essential for her survival, carry great risks for the woman. These are the risks of internalization. Enforced obedience possesses the woman because she enacts, in her bodySelf, that which the rapist demands. As part of her behavioral patterns of actions, she internalizes the rules and structures of the situation which has entrapped her. Once made physically obedient during rape's assault on her bodySelf, she is in great danger of becoming psychologically obedient. Internalizing the rapist's rule over her, she becomes bound to him. For example, when rapists insist that women not tell anyone about the rape, many women comply for years.

Once raped, the rape event has colonized the woman's mind. Rape now exists in her mind just as it once existed in her body. The binding power of the rapist's demand for obedience during rape are evident in the woman's reactions after rape. She does not easily remember nor resolve her anxious memories of the bodily assault. It is also, I believe, equally difficult for her to remember and resolve her memories of her own compliance behaviors during rape. Women, after rape, make many self-judging comments about their own choices of submission during rape.[14]

Obedience and disobedience, while appearing in common-sense to be polar opposites, do not physically function in such a dualistic manner. The more tightly controlled the interpersonal field of interaction in which obedience is commanded, the more obedience and disobedience merge into dysfunctionality. Once a forceful and binding command has been issued, both disobedience or obedience behaviors reinforce the power of the command. The command's power cancels the recipient's power. Demands for obedience during rape disempower the woman in a recursive structure[15] that strangles her own agency. No matter what behavior she chooses, she is bound by the command.

All and any responses, no matter what their nature, reinforce the power of the man. In a rape interaction, the man is the agent of absolute, omnipotent power. In situations of rape, the man reflects cultural patterns of male dominance in ways that their central dynamic cannot be missed. Rape is about men's total, unwavering demands for women's obedience and submission. Rape is about the theft of power from women to enhance men's power over them.

The function of obedience commands during rape are to colonize the woman's body and her will. They separate the woman from her own self-controlled agency. Trapped within the rapist's field of commands, the woman is bound to the rapist. She is not free to ignore the command or to transform it.

Rape events become a recursive, shattering hall of mirrors in women's life stories. The recursive nature of obedience demands continue their control of women's psyches long after the rape event is past. In this dismembering hall of mirrors, each mirror both reflects and distorts cultural messages about female obedience and male dominance.

Rape, begun as an event of terror for the woman in which she must obey one man in order to survive, becomes embedded within her consciousness and relationality. Her experiences during rape refract and distill her own personal collection of experiences, stories, and values about women's obedience to men's individual and collective power over her.

RECOVERY AND HOPE:
SHATTERING THE RECURSIVE EPISTEMOLOGY OF RAPE COMMANDS

One task of women in recovery from rape is to relearn empowerment of the will to act in self-protection. She will need to learn how to resist the rape which lives on inside her mind. Because of rape's intimate ties to bodily awareness and kinesthetic sensation, and because of the presence of terror which may or may not have been dissociated, the woman cannot simply forget her rape and resume her life as if nothing had happened to her.

The woman will need, instead, to integrate rape's historical presence within her life story. To move out of the postrape crisis into an embodied wholeness of spirit, body, emotion, cognition, and relationality, she needs to learn ways of confronting the ongoing cultural story of woman's desired obedience to men. Sensitized to sexual violence because of her own experiences, she must learn how to recognize and handle cultural injunctions to men about the desirability of rape. She needs to learn how to survive additional events in her ongoing life that appear to structurally function like rape in their limitation of her personal agency.

The woman must learn, according to Janeway[16] to distrust, disbelieve, and withdraw consent. Her first act of disbelief is her refusal to accept the definition of her bodySelf as put forth by her violator. Even when she has been terrorized into total immobility during rape, she can begin, after rape, once more to claim her own agency.

It seems to me, in patriarchal cultures which teach, encourage, and promote the rape of women, that the spiritual journey of any woman must include extensive journeys into distrust, disbelief and withdrawal of consent. Any cultural teaching which advocates women's desired subjugation by the man must be deconstructed so that the woman is empowered to shatter the force of that teaching from within. In looking at rape as the extreme example of woman's submission and obedience, we have found a recursive epistemology that binds the woman to the man and his violence and denies to her, her own agency in the world.

Our task as theologians within the peace church tradition is to begin to re-think obedience teachings in our common life together. If we want women to be full participants in God's creative order, then our task is to begin an active dismantling process of all structures and teachings which insist that women must obey men. I think, for example, that it is quite likely that all headship theologies need the rape of women in order to maintain theological obedience structures for women in religious life.

Our resistance to changing our collective moments of worship is another sign to me of the struggles ahead in changing our communal experiences of patriarchal, ideological Christianity into the more inclusive practice promised by the apostle Paul, in which there is no male nor female, no slave nor freeperson in our experience of being the unified people of God.

As long as our worship almost exclusively focuses either on

the monarchical and hierarchical images of God as Lord and King or on the parental images of God as Father or on the syntax issues of the divine as He, there will be women in search of healing who are re-wounded each gathering time by our patterns of Christian worship. If these kinds of cultural and theological structures remain in place, the rape of women will continue.

In a century which has begun to reveal the depth and breadth of abuse in families, I think it is quite likely that we should begin to reserve parental images of God for our private spirituality. The Jewish text and the Christian text are incredibly rich with diverse metaphors for God. We do not need to be limited to parental language in our communal worship. Because men and women both batter and molest children, I believe we should, in our communal worship, stop using all familial metaphors for the divine presence who enters our life as friend, as comforter, as breath of God, as companion, etc. For some men and women, God as mother is as alienating as God as father is for some other women and men. Depending on who the abusive person was in their own childhood, they may stumble and fall over the linguistic metaphors we use to think about the indescribable, the ineffable, the unknown. To insist, collectively, upon our historical privileges in worship, is to insist upon the continuing alienation for some of the survivors of sexual and physical abuse.

Even at this suggestion, many of you are experiencing the loss of language which has sustained you. To not communally call on God as our mother or as our father is, perhaps, akin to the death of God's relationship with us. We feel the loss of something that most comforts us in worship.

Perhaps that is the act of solidarity with survivors of abuse which we must make. If my insistence upon naming God as mother or as father, alienates my sister or brother who was battered, molested, or raped, then I must be willing to be led into the communal search for inclusive metaphors for God, those which all of us can share. To celebrate the divine presence in each of our lives demands that the body of Christ include all those who have stated their belief in Jesus and their intent to live a Christian life. To conduct communal worship services that re-wound the Christian survivor of sexual or physical abuse is to deny that we are the body of Christ in our gathered worship.

In my private need, however, when God comes to seek me out in the privacy of my inwardness, God can become mommy, daddy, lover, monarch, or ruler. There where my personal need can be most transparent and most hidden, in that paradoxical action of the Holy Spirit as revealer, critic, and best friend, I can return to being God's daughter.

The contemporary hymn writer, Brian Wren, has been struggling with his own images of God in his desire to include all men and women in communal worship. His hymn "God of Many Name,"[17] explores the concept of God's multiple names. He uses the liturgical practice of hymn singing to teach us something in worship, something that we so often and so easily forget, that our names for God can become idolatrous if we claim the human power to insist that our individual or communal naming of God is the only possible naming of God.

The woman, after rape, will encounter many such re-woundings in a rape-prone culture. The woman, to heal herself after rape and to bring her newSelf[18] into birth, will need to challenge all teachings about obedience structures. She will need to learn how to shatter the recursive epistemology from within so that she can free her bodySelf from the rapist's commands and their continuing demands upon her life.

As peace church theologians, clinicians, ministers, concerned laypersons and educators, we can choose to assist her in her journey towards wholeness. We can be present at the birthing of the new bodySelf as midwives and helpers. Or we can abandon her to the kinds of theology and ideology which continue her enslavement within patriarchal cultures. Without our help, some women will be strong enough to reach into their own psychic vaginas to birth a new bodySelf. But many more such births will be stillborn.

We must now recognize, I believe, that our historical theologies of obedience have not called women into Christ's freedom. Rather, these theologies and ideologies have bound women to men who have dominated them and violated them. Christendom's ideology of women's inferiority and its teachings about the necessity of women's subservience to men has reaped a harvest of unprecedented violence in women's lives. No woman here is safe from the rapist's behavioral enactment of the ideology of dominance. Today's criminal statistics in the United States indicate that one woman in four will be sexually assaulted during her lifetime. We know that age does not make a difference (literature reveals an age span of 2 months to 93 years of age); that religion does not make a difference (religious campuses have as much date rape as do secular ones); race or ethnicity do not make a difference (rape tends to be enacted within one's own ethnic or racial groupings); that geography does not make a difference (rural areas and cities are both having rape epidemics).

A satisfying peace theology must make way for the woman who has been raped to enter liminal space and transform her life.

We must get out of her way so she can become whole once more. We must also work at changing our ideas about the desirability of male dominance in all our relationships as men and women so that rape will end. Until our theology, ideology, worship practices, and worldview change, rape will continue its progressive disempowerment of all women's lives. Christendom's historical teachings about men's necessary dominance over women, are, to me, no longer the gospel.

NOTES

1. This is my term for the Self as defined by Mary Daly: "The original core of one's being that cannot be contained [or possessed]" with the addition of the woman's body as an aspect of the Self.

2. *Diving Deep and Surfacing*, (Boston: Beacon Press, 1980).

3. *The Journey is Home*. (Boston: Beacon Press, 1985).

4. *Women's Reality*. (Minneapolis: Winston Press, 1981).

5. "Sexual Violence." Paper presented as part of the Harvard Medical School Department of Continuing Education conference, Learning From Women, Boston, April 1987.

6. *Women Hating*. (New York: Dutton, 1974) and *Pornography: Men Possessing Women*. (New York: Perigree, 1981).

7. *Violence Against Women and the Ongoing Challenge to Racism*. (Latham, NY: Kitchen Table/Women of Color Press, 1985).

8. Peggy Reeves Sanday, *Female Power and Male Dominance*. (Cambridge: Cambridge University Press, 1981).

9. Mary Daly with Jane Caputi. *Webster's First New Intergalactic Wickedary of the English Language*. (Boston: Beacon Press, 1987) 87.

10. Vern Bullough with Bonnie Bullough, *The Subordinate Sex: A History of Attitudes Towards Women*. (Chicago: University of Illinois Press, 1974); Rosemary Radford Ruether, *Religion and Sexism: Images of Women in the Jewish and Christian Traditions*. (New York: Simon and Schuster, 1974); and W. E. Phipps, *Influential Theologians on Wo/man*. (Washington, DC: University Press of America, 1980).

11. Phyllis Trible, *Texts of Terror: Feminist Readings of Biblical Narratives*. (Philadelphia: Fortress, 1984).

12. Rosemary Radford Ruether, *Contemporary Roman Catholicism: Crises and Challenges*. (Kansas City: Sheed and Ward, 1987).

13. *Truth or Dare: Encounters With Power, Authority, and Mystery*. (San Francisco: Harper and Row, 1988).

14. R. Januff-Bulan, "Characterological Versus Behavioral Self Blame: Inquiries into Depression and Rape." *Journal of Personality and Social Psychology* 37(10), 1979, 1798-1809; "Esteem and Control Bases of Blame: Adaptive Strategies for Victims Versus Observers. *Journal of Personality* 50 (2), 1982 180-192; and with Fieze, I. H. "A Theoretical Model for Understanding Victimization." *Journal of Social Issues* 39 (2), 1983, 1-17. See also, J. H. Katz, *No Fairy Godmothers, No Magic Wands: The Healing Process After Rape*. (Saratoga, CA: R and E Publishers, 1984).

15. A term used by Gregory Bateson is "The Birth of a Matrix or Double Bind and Epistemology," in M. M. Berger, ed. *Beyond the Bouble Bind* (New York: Bruner/Mazel, 1978), 39-64.

16. E. Janeway. *Powers of the Weak*. (New York: Knopf, 1981).

17. *The United Methodist Hymnal* (1989). (Nashville: The United Methodist Publishing House).

18. See footnote 1 above for the sense of Self here.

RESPONSE

Miriam E. Martin

I applaud Ruth's wisdom and insight in dealing with a most difficult topic in a sensitive and scholarly manner.

Much of what I have to say relates to my re-entry into Mennonite circles. I am seeking to clarify the essence of my theological heritage in relation to my increasing awareness of the evil in so-called good environments. I do not come to you as a theologian, nor can I share a personal story of healing from rape. However, I am a woman, a nurse and a feminist. I have had a variety of experiences with the white male patriarchy both in society and in the Mennonite church. I have often experienced the command to obey in ways that dis-membered and devalued my personhood and my faith experience.

I have experienced invisibility from both men and women who disregarded my views and experiences because they were expressed by a female who had feminist views that were not in line with the patriarchal views of the day. On the other hand, I have also experienced deep caring from brothers and sisters at times of personal brokenness and dis-memberment. So, I have known pain and I have known healing.

THE ISSUE OF OBEDIENCE

From infancy we as Mennonite women have been taught to obey those in authority. When we were old enough to understand, we were taught to "obey God rather than man." At the same time, we were taught to call God father, thus equating God with male authority figures in our lives. If we were taught that obedience does not allow for questioning the orders delivered by authority, we were then set up to "be and become" in response to others' wishes and needs rather than our own internal drives and strivings. This command to obey controlled all aspects of our lives and development. If we resisted, asked questions, or blatantly disobeyed, we were judged and punished in some way. Sometimes the punishment involved withholding of love. This reinforced a sense of self-blame and unworthiness.

Yet, our theology says that God is a loving God, and God does not ask us to do more than we are able to do. How does this all fit together?

RAPE PRONE CULTURE

Ruth's paper describes ours as a rape-prone culture. I believe there are two issues which the church must deal with within this culture: First, there is a lack of clarity about the meaning of sexuality. (Remember: rape is not about sex, it is about power.) And second, we live in a patriarchy. This environment places godlike authority in the hands of the male.

1. The Meaning of Sexuality

While I was in my church-shopping mode last year, I visited a local Mennonite church where the minister told the congregation that the sex act is the most sacred demonstration of intimacy in a relationship. He said this while he was trying to teach teenagers to "wait until marriage" to practice sex.

I have real problems with this view. In a healthy, intimate relationship, the sex act is part of the intimacy, but not necessarily the deepest aspect of intimacy. The writers of *Human Sexuality in the Christian Life* said, "Human health and wholeness do not require genital relations. Sex we can live without; what we cannot live without is intimacy...Intimacy is closeness, familiarity, trust, friendship. It is mutual acceptance and understanding. It is the willingness to be open and vulnerable to another person...It is caring and being cared for in return."[1]

I would define sexuality as the interaction of one's sexual identity (gender identity, self-esteem, body image), sex act, and sex drive. It is expressed through biological and psycho-social means. An alteration in any aspect of sexuality can alter the manner in which it is expressed.[2]

There is a belief in our culture that the *sex drive* cannot be controlled, especially by men. Yet science tells us that sex drive is a "learned response that originates in the cerebral cortex." The patriarchy supports the notion that rape is sex and men have the right to demonstrate their power over women in this way.

Just as the sex drive is learned, *sex acts* are also learned within the sociocultural context. So men and women who grow up in a patriarchal culture learn that forced sex is a male right. Yet, the woman's experience of this act is that it is wrong, painful, and dehumanizing.

What do we, Christians who believe in peace and justice, have to say to this cultural norm? Although Ruth said rape is part of a rape-prone culture, I still believe that rape is a violent act committed by an emotionally ill or immature person who uses sex acts as instruments of violence. Rape should never be seen as sexual activity or expression.

On the other hand, rape is part of the larger violence picture. Research findings support the notion that violence and violent behaviors are learned. "Social learning theory postulates that a child learns to be violent in the family setting in which a violent parent has been taken as a role model...This exposure teaches both the means and the approval of violence."[3] I would extend this notion to say that violent behaviors are learned and supported in our society, and that much of church life is patterned after the model of surrounding society.

2. Living in a Patriarchy

We need to deal frontally with the patriarchal society issue. Christian women do not live in a vacuum. They consult secular literature in their desire to understand the incongruities in their lives. It is clear that the patriarchy is a serious problem in both church and society as we examine the question of rape. As long as women are viewed as property, as subhuman and undesirable, women will be raped and have other dehumanizing atrocities perpetrated upon them.

In many ways we are all in bondage to the patriarchy. How do we break the bonds and find wholeness? All efforts to break out are a threat to the integrity of the patriarchal system. And, even the best intentioned people (men and women) use various methods (often unknown to themselves) to maintain the system and the bondage.

Does Matthew 18 apply here? What does it mean that the church has the power to bind and the power to loose? Have we abdicated this God-given power?

HEALING THE CHURCH

We need to change the myths of the church in relation to sexuality and the patriarchy.

1. Revaluing Sexuality.

The first step in redefining sexuality is to accept our own sexuality. We must believe and see, as Mary Schertz put it, "the blessedness of being created female, an image of the divine; the blessedness of being male, an image of the divine."[4] Sex is to be viewed as a gift from God to be enjoyed, not abused. Such a revaluing of our sexuality might lead us to equalize the categories of sin. Is "sexual sin" a bigger sin than gluttony, gossip, or greed? We need to clarify the difference between right relationship sexual practice and sexual violence. Anything that devalues the personhood of someone, from verbal slurs to rape, is not right relationship sexual practice.

2. Dismantling the Patriarchy.

Ruth says we need "to begin an active dismantling process of all structures and teaching which insist that women must obey men." One approach would be to practice "holy disobedience." (This may be the same as the "redemptive resistance" suggested by Gayle Gerber Koontz.)

I recognize that this is a paradoxical concept. It is as though I am saying there is such a thing as sacred sinning. We need to learn to value self even though the patriarchy supports the opposite view. We must claim our freedom and equality in Christ.

Ruth reminded us that Christianity has been dominated by White Male theological interpretations for centuries. It is amazing to me that women have not bolted from the church en masse. Is it because we have bought the White Male System, or is it because we see beyond the male interpretations to the reality of the Christian message?

What did Christ teach by his example about the value of women? According to Scanzoni and Hardesty,[5] "He simply treated women as humans." (See Luke 10:38-42; 21:1-4; John 4; Matthew 27:55, etc.)

Do we have the responsibility to confront those among us who do not treat women as fully human? How should that confrontation happen? I believe that these broader issues need to be addressed if we are to learn how to be effective with victims of rape, and if we are to be able to provide a safe environment in which healing can occur.

HEALING THE VICTIM

Ruth has told us that healing is the goal for women who have been shattered or dis-membered by the violence of rape. She has clarified for us that healing begins to happen as a broken person seeks healing, and that healing and wholeness are really synonyms. What is our responsibility as caring sisters and brothers to provide an environment which assists the broken person to want to seek healing? What beliefs and actions are essential to provide a healing environment?

Ruth has told us that for healing to happen, "the woman must journey into and through her awareness of rage-filled grief for the lost or destroyed bodySelf." That journey is full of anger, pain, self-doubt, fear, shame, self-blame, grief and sadness, and unreality. How comfortable are we with these essential emotional experiences? How prepared are we to walk with the wounded one on her journey to wholeness?

Once this most blatant violence against a woman has occurred, the emotions related to having been violated never totally disappear. There are longterm effects. The traumatic event is re-experienced in flashbacks, nightmares and/or feelings of guilt, decreased self-confidence, and the need to place blame on self or others. Common health professional diagnoses for this syndrome are *post-trauma response* and *post traumatic stress disorder*.

I believe that nonjudgmental presencing or empathic "with-ness" is the essential act which must be present for healing processes to be supported. This empathic with-ness must be a part of every aspect of the assistance of a victim of rape. Gerber Koontz reminded us that compassion is empowering. I believe the concept of nonjudgmental with-ness can instruct our theology. Block told us to let people tell us what their experience is, and Edmunds suggested we should use power in the service of life.

Empathic with-ness includes active listening, not touching or not touching inappropriately, helping the person talk about the event, sharing one's own struggle with the meaning of the event as appropriate, assisting in practicing assertive communication, staying with the person, especially during high anxiety times, and supporting the expression of emotions--anger, fear, rage--as normal and appropriate.

Space does not permit an adequate treatment of the subject here, but it is important that health care practitioners and other helpers are thoroughly trained in relating to rape victims so that they are not revictimized by an insensitive system.[6]

CONCLUSION

I believe that practicing Anabaptist Christians are called to work out their faith, to be accountable for their relationships with God, fellow Christians, and humanity in general. I believe that practicing one's faith involves a daily walk, and a daily dose of God's grace. It involves recognizing our own imperfections. I know this personally. I did not experience physical or sexual violence in my family of origin or in the intimate relationships in my adult life. But

I have often experienced psychological violence--and I know how to be a perpetrator of psychological violence. I became acutely aware of this as I learned to own and process anger. My empathy for victim and perpetrator has been enhanced by my increasing awareness of my own imperfections.

But I can also claim God's grace as I seek forgiveness from the ones I have hurt. In this context, I still strongly believe that as we walk a lifelong walk of faith, our growth and insight have value in dialogue with fellow believers as we are all "on the way." It is through this process that we can move toward solutions to the difficult problems we are discussing here.

NOTES

1. Wilmer Martin and Sue Goertzen, *Human Sexuality in the Christian Life: A Working Document for Study and Dialogue.* (Newton, Kansas: Faith and Life Press, and Scottdale, Pa.: Mennonite Publishing House, 1985).

2. For the concepts in this definition I am indebted to Sheryl Miller's unpublished thesis, "The Expression of Sexuality in the Female Geron" University of Iowa, 1977.

3. Joan L. Creasia and Barbara Parker, *Conceptual Foundations of Professional Nursing Practice* (St. Louis: Mosby Year Book, 1991), 425.

4. See her article in this volume.

5. *All We're Meant to Be: A Biblical Approach to Women's Liberation*, (Waco, Texas: Word Books, 1975).

6. A good, thorough presentation is to be found in Bonnie Wesorick, *Standards of Nursing Care: A Model for Clinical Practice.* (Philadelphia: J.B. Lippincott, 1990), 255-256.

CONTENT TO SUFFER: AN EXPLORATION OF MENNONITE THEOLOGY FROM THE CONTEXT OF VIOLENCE AGAINST WOMEN

Carol Penner

How do Mennonite women respond to the suffering which results from living in a sexist world? How will we react to being battered by a husband, raped by a boyfriend, molested by an uncle or humiliated by a sexist remark on the street? Our decisions will be influenced at least in part by our theology. Mennonite theology has generally not explicitly addressed the context of women's suffering, yet women have always turned to their faith to find hope, meaning and the strength to carry on. But all too often Mennonite teaching on the subject of suffering has conveyed a message which disempowers women suffering from patriarchal violence, destroying their hope and spreading confusion rather than understanding. For example, in Mennonite theology little effort has been made to distinguish between different kinds of suffering, between the pain of sickness and the pain of sexual assault, the anguish of natural disaster and the anguish of family breakdown. The common message in Mennonite thought is often that suffering, all suffering, should simply be endured, just as Jesus endured the cross.[1]

This theology is not good news for people who have been abused. A theology is needed which does not see all suffering as redemptive, which proclaims liberation from oppression, and which encourages faithful women to seek an end to their suffering. In this paper I will explore some aspects of Mennonite theology in terms of suffering, suggesting some directions which would reflect the context of violence against women.

Where does our theology of suffering originate? There are many routes one could follow in trying to uncover how Mennonite women learn to make sense of suffering. In my own experience I can see that my theology was formed in a myriad of ways. Initially I learned at home. Living with a grandmother who had survived the Russian Revolution undoubtedly affected me, as did the death through illness of both of my parents. Sunday school and girl's club, young people's group and catechism class were all formative. I don't remember explicit teaching on the subject of suffering, but I remember a poster I hung on my wall as a child which said "Bloom where you are planted" and the songs I sang to myself assured me that "Jesus wants me for a sunbeam" and that "smilers never lose and frowners never win." I read a lot of devotional literature as I grew older, and theological studies in my undergraduate years exposed me to some Mennonite theologians who were very influential in my thinking. Significant people and events shaped my theology, and readings in feminist theory often challenged much of what I had earlier believed.

This existential blending of formal and popular theology is something which I want to reflect in this paper. A historical study of early Anabaptist views of suffering, or an essay which examines how our history as a Mennonite people has influenced our theology would be fascinating, but in this paper I have chosen to paint with broader strokes. Similarly, an in-depth discussion of one theologian's work would provide interesting material. I do believe the work of professional theologians is important, yet when discussing their work, there is the danger of assuming that Mennonites believe (let alone read) what their theologians write. To avoid this danger, one can turn to more popular theology as it is expressed in worship services, Sunday school material, catechism or church newspapers. In doing this, however, one risks overlooking a consistent and systematic treatment of the subject which the academic venue affords.

Keeping this tension in mind, I have chosen to discuss three sources which I believe illustrate Mennonite perspectives on suffering: a worship resource, a book of theology and a sample of publications by Mennonite Central Committee. I have chosen these three sources because of their influence in my own life and with the hope that they will be evocative, prompting persons at this conference to examine their own experiences and the sources which have been formative in their own theologizing. I will end by discussing some insights gleaned from feminist theology on the topic of suffering, as a way of suggesting directions which I think are proving helpful for Mennonite women.

SOURCE ONE

As a member of a Mennonite church, every Sunday I join in the worship of God through song. I often ask myself, "Do I believe what I am singing?" Music is an important element of Mennonite worship, and the hymns that we sing articulate and shape our theological understanding. *The Mennonite Hymnal*[2] is a frequently used book in many congregations, and its compilers understood the pedagogical function which hymns often have. In their introduction they state that the texts were examined for their "theological appropriateness" and their "present pertinence."[3] In this section I will examine the theology of suffering which is reflected in these hymns.[4]

The theme of suffering is one that is certainly present in many hymns in *The Mennonite Hymnal*. The hymns convey the belief that God sees both the oppressor and the oppressed,[5] and is near whenever Christians suffer.[6] Several hymns emphasize that God's presence is a source of comfort.

> He comes with succor speedy
> To those who suffer wrong;
> To help the poor and needy,
> And bid the weak be strong...[7]

Christians are urged to remember that "the Lord is on thy side."[8]

The *Hymnal*, however, interprets God's presence in a way which minimizes the pain of suffering. Pain is seen to fly away before the presence of God; anguish melts away,[9] and the Christian can even "smile at pain while Thou art near."[10] Poetic license could excuse some of this minimization, but the consistency of this denial of pain makes a clear theological statement. The sufferer finds such solace in God that suffering no longer is an issue:

> On Thee we fling our burd'ning woe,
> O Love divine, forever dear,
> Content to suffer, while we know,
> Living and dying, Thou are near.[11]

In these hymns the Christian response to suffering is to be not only one of passive acceptance, but even joyful obedience.

Some hymns go so far as to suggest that suffering originates from God as a type of punishment, as in a hymn which refers to God's chastening rod,[12] or the lines "Let sorrow do its work, Send grief and pain..."[13] Other hymns are more ambiguous about the origin of suffering, but suggest that the Christian should be "Content, whatever lot I see, Since 'tis my God that leadeth me."[14]

Suffering is often mentioned in the context of discipleship, and bearing the cross.[15] Jesus followed a path of suffering, and Christians are urged to trace the footsteps of Jesus, being meek and forgiving, humbly bearing the scorns and scoffs of men.[16] In the face of abuse Christians should be loving and merciful, and "Glad with the [Jesus] to suffer pain."[17] The pain of the Christian is made more bearable through remembering the pain that Jesus suffered.[18]

The only relief from suffering offered, other than the presence of God which supposedly takes away pain, is the relief which comes from death and entrance to heaven:

> Be still, my soul! The hour is hast'ning on
> When we shall be forever with the Lord,
> When disappointment, grief, and fear are gone,

Sorrow forgot, love's purest joys restored.[19]
The idea that heaven will bring relief from pain was reiterated at many points.

Mennonite women who have suffered under patriarchal violence have sung these hymns for years: it is impossible to know the pain and confusion which may have been compounded by the theology which these hymns profess. It may very well be that the authors of the hymns had in mind physical suffering due to illness when they wrote their hymns, or perhaps they were speaking of the spiritual pain of separation from God.[20] The intentions of the authors, however, do not preclude people from applying these hymns to their own circumstances, and the circumstances of abuse occur with great frequency. Admittedly, the *Hymnal's* message that God is present with Christians who suffer is a comforting one for women who have been abused. However, the majority of hymns convey a message which is not good news for women.

This brief exploration of the *Hymnal* suggests that while it does not address the issue of violence against women specifically, its theology conveys a definite message to women within that context. The message is to endure suffering, not to complain, and to be comforted by God's presence in the midst of suffering. Some hymns reinforce the idea that suffering is God-given and tolerable if one only has enough faith. Nowhere does the hymnal suggest that suffering is not always part of God's plan for the Christian, or that Christians might be called to liberation from suffering in certain situations.

SOURCE TWO

Not many Mennonites read theology books, but if they do, one of the books they are likely to read is the popular *Politics of Jesus* by John Howard Yoder.[21] It is frequently used as a text in Mennonite colleges, and for many people it may be their only exposure to Mennonite academic theology. In this section I will consider what message this book gives to women who are suffering from patriarchal violence. Obviously, I am not providing a systematic treatment of Yoder's view of suffering. However the popularity of the book warrants a perusal of its view of suffering, while keeping in mind that the theologian's larger body of work would provide a more nuanced and accurate view of Yoder's theology.

The Politics of Jesus, Yoder addresses the theme of suffering at some length. The purpose of the book is to establish the normativity of Jesus' life and death for contemporary social ethics; in Yoder's view an important component of Jesus' life was his willingness to suffer (23). Christians suffer when they follow Jesus' example of loving the enemy and praying for the abuser. Just as the cross was the logical outcome of Jesus' life as he resisted the powers in his society, so suffering will also be the cost of social nonconformity for Christians (97).

Yoder is careful not to condone all suffering as redemptive. Suffering is not good in and of itself, nor is it chosen as a tool to obtain the conversion of the abuser. He differentiates between suffering as Jesus did and suffering for some other reason. The cross is not random suffering which the Christian must endure, such as sickness or catastrophe (97). Rather, suffering can be cross-like only if it is freely chosen, innocent, and a result of the evil of adversaries (132).

Yoder uses the term "revolutionary subordination" to describe the meaning of the cross. As a citizen of God's kingdom, Jesus was genuinely free of the powers of the world, powers being the religious, intellectual, moral and social structures originally ordained by God, but now fallen and corrupted (146). To show his humanness, however, Jesus allowed himself to be subordinate to the powers that existed, accepting even his own death at their hands. Jesus' cross represented his victory over the powers of the world (148).

Christians too, Yoder suggests, must be subordinate to these God-ordained but now corrupted earthly powers, even if they prevent people from living as free human beings (144). Submission to these powers is possible "...in view of the relative unimportance of such social distinctions when seen in the light of the coming fulfillment of God's purposes" (187).

Yoder's theology of suffering as it is expressed in *The Politics of Jesus* seems to be particularly bad news to women who suffer abuse. The books seems to support the position of the many Mennonite women who remain in abusive relationships out of a sincere desire to convert their husbands through love. Yoder does make a distinction between voluntary and involuntary suffering, stating that only voluntary suffering is Christ-like. Feminists would suggest that women do not choose to be abused, that their suffering is involuntary, and thus *feminist* victims of abuse would not interpret their suffering as Christ-like. However, the interpretation *many* women have of their own situation is that they are choosing to accept abuse just as Jesus accepted the cross. Yoder's book would seem to support their decision to remain in abusive relationships.

Indeed, Yoder' discussion of the "powers of the world" would bolster such a tragic reading of his book. Yoder never explicitly says whether patriarchy is one of the social structures ordained by God to which the Christian should be subordinate. However, patriarchal authority is a system which has often been seen as God-ordained and indeed, Yoder's own discussion of the Haustafeln would not contradict such a belief.[22] Undoubtedly many Mennonite women have endured abuse because they submitted themselves to what they believed was the God-given authority of the male members of the household. Yoder's book provides no corrective to such thinking.

SOURCE THREE

We sing our theology, we read our theology, and we live out our theology; therefore, it is appropriate to examine the service arm of the church in the form of Mennonite Central Committee. While academically trained theologians have been silent on the issue of patriarchal violence, several MCC publications have addressed the suffering of women in some very practical ways. This is a hopeful sign. The work and publications of this agency provide a valuable theological resource for many people, particularly for women who are experiencing suffering. Two of these publications which reflect the actions of Mennonites in the area of women's suffering are the *Women's Concerns Report* and *The Purple Packet*.

Women's Concerns Report has been in existence since 1973. Edited and written by women, each issue is composed of short article which center around a theme or issue which women have found important. Several issues of this now bi-monthly publication have been specifically devoted to the question of the abuse of women. As early as 1978 two issues of the report concerned family violence, while a more recent issue in 1987 looked specifically at the subject of wife abuse. Other *Reports* have looked at issues of pornography, racism, and ageism as they affect women.

Women's Concerns Report makes a theological statement by its very existence. It proclaims that women's voices are important and that women's perspectives on their own reality need to be recorded. In the pages of the *Report*, women's suffering is taken seriously and there is space given for women to express their pain, their anger, their sorrow. Individual stories are set within the wider framework which social analysis provides. Significantly, the *Report* provides a forum for women to explore the theological meaning of their experiences. This process of theological reflection is seen clearly in the March-April 1989 issue on incest edited by Ethel Y. Metzler. In it incest survivors themselves tell the stories of abuse and the meaning that this abuse has had for their lives. A brief survey of statistics sets the problem in a wider framework, biblical reflection on reconciliation and shalom, pastoral concerns in ministering to survivors and a list of resources are also included. Reader's letters in subsequent *Reports* suggest that many found it very helpful. Another publication which reflects how Mennonites are working to end violence against women is *The Purple Packet*, a compilation of resources collected for the education of clergy and lay people concerned about the issue of wife abuse. A product of the Mennonite Central Committee's "Domestic Violence Taskforce", *The Purple Packet* takes the context of abuse seriously.

Like *Women's Concerns Report*, an important component of *The Purple Packet* is storytelling. The stories show that people experiencing family violence are confronted by "...basic questions about the meaning of life and God's role in our human suffering."[23] *The Packet* contains practical advice for pastors confronted with this suffering, as well as a handbook for the survivor herself entitled "You Are Not Alone."

The handbook, as well as other resources in *The Packet*, provides social analysis about the causes of women's suffering, pointing out that violence against women is a societal problem which exhibits itself through individuals. Connections are drawn between male and female role socialization, the economic inequality of men and women, and societal attitudes which have viewed the family as a private unit. These are all symptoms of the patriarchal system which underlies the abuse of women.

The Purple Packet also contains several excellent theological articles drawn from the ecumenical community. Unfortunately, none are by Mennonites, since virtually nothing has been written on the subject by Mennonite theologians. There is an urgent need for reflection on violence against women from a peace church perspective.

DIRECTIONS FOR MENNONITE THEOLOGY

As *The Purple Packet* illustrates, Mennonites who are concerned about the theological significance of violence against women are utilizing the rich and growing ecumenical body of literature on this issue. Several authors have emerged in recent years who name violence against women as the specific context out of which they theologize. It is to these resources which I will now turn, focussing on two directions which can be instructive for us as we seek to make Mennonite theology more relevant to the experience of women. The first direction is in terms of theological method. In feminist theology women set the agenda, defining their own problems and suggesting their own theological responses. The second direction which Mennonites need to consider is the message of feminist theology which encourages women to work for freedom from oppression.

The feminist theologians who speak to the context of
women's suffering are primarily women. Many of them speak from
direct experience, either as survivors of abuse themselves or as
pastors and counselors of battered women.[24] The method is clear:
women must theologize about the lives of women. The Mennonite
church is leaning in this direction as was evidenced by the MCC
documents considered earlier. This conference is another example
of this change in direction: women are beginning to shape the
theological agenda of the Mennonite church.

Feminist theologians claim the right to include their stories,
and their interpretations of their stories, as part of their method of
theological reflection. In terms of women's suffering, feminist
theologians suggest that women need to reject what they have been
taught is a "proper" response to their suffering. Our cultural and
religious traditions give women both direct and subtle messages that
they are to be silent about the suffering they experience.[25] Mennonite culture is no different in this respect. Di Brandt, a Mennonite poet from Manitoba, writes in this regard:

> I feel so much anger for the way we were made to suffer, as
> children, as women, swallowing our desires in secret, submit-
> ting to the will of the fathers and God and fate, learning our
> own silence. I feel so angry when I see Mennonite women
> trying to forget (blank out) their lives as they grow old,
> because there was so much suffering in them, the way they
> have learned at great cost *not to speak.*[26]

The Mennonite theological tradition has supported this culture
which has silenced women. This is reflected in the lack of theological writing on women's suffering[27] and its absence from the peace
studies curricula at Mennonite schools and colleges. This must
change.

As women begin to break the silence which surrounds abuse,
they will begin to name the significance of their own suffering. For
example, in the case of sexual assault, Marie Fortune suggests that
this type of violation makes clear the totality of the violation of the
person: "Being forced sexually against one's will is the ultimate
experience of powerlessness, short of death."[28] This is in marked
contrast to the way male theologians have sometimes minimized sexual assault (on the rare occasion that they do mention it). For example, John Howard Yoder in his discussion of assault in his book
What Would You Do?, brackets the question of "sexual menace" as
an irrelevant emotional element which clouds a rational discussion
of assault.[29] As Mennonite theology becomes more open to the
voices of women, it will reflect the anger and pain which many Mennonite women feel.

The methods which feminist theologians employ invariably involve social analysis as they look to the causes, not just to the symptoms of women's suffering. This method was also evidenced in the *Women's Concerns Report*. Feminists point to the gender-based ordering of power and authority which pervades all aspects of our society and which leads inevitably to the abuse of women.[30] They call this system "patriarchy". Its symptoms are as widespread and varied as pornography, sexist language, gender discrimination in the workplace and the division of paid and unpaid labor in our society. Feminists also explore the connection between sexism and racism and the effects this has on women.[31] Feminists refuse to see women's suffering as a series of isolated tragedies. This poses a challenge for feminists working in the Mennonite church. Our task should not simply be to hear and mend the suffering of individual women, but also to engage in a wholesale critique of Mennonite family and church structures which perpetuate the suffering of women.

Feminist theology contains a message of liberation. This message is conveyed in different ways. Phyllis Trible, for example, explores biblical texts which invite repentance as a means of educating the church about women's suffering.[32] Other theologians concentrate on providing worship resources which proclaim the liberation from suffering under patriarchy.[33]

One way that liberation is conveyed is through discussions about Jesus and his normativity as a role model. This area is of particular concern to Mennonites, as our theology of suffering is often christologically based (as was illustrated above). Feminists are in agreement that there has been an overemphasis on servanthood and self-sacrifice, particularly for women. Where feminists part ways, however, is over how radical a critique of Christianity is necessary.

Women suffering from abuse, some feminists argue, can be liberated by a careful reading of Scripture. The overemphasis on suffering and the crucifixion needs to be balanced with the victory of the resurrection.[34] Others argue that the main symbols of Christianity promote abuse. These arguments are put forward most powerfully by Brown and Parker in the anthology *Christianity, Patriarchy and Abuse*. They suggest that the central image of Christ on the cross conveys the unacceptable message that suffering is redemptive:

> Despite all the correctives taught by liberation theology on how to interpret suffering, this Christian theology with atonement at the center still encourages martyrdom and victimization...Our internalization of this theology traps us in an almost unbreakable cycle of abuse.[35]

These theological differences reflect the experiences of abused women, some of whom have found comfort in Christian symbols, while others have found them to be relentlessly oppressive. What perspectives will Mennonite peace theologians bring to this dialogue?

CONCLUSION

In this paper I have attempted to touch on a few Mennonite sources which have shaped my own thinking about suffering. My theology has been shaped by the hymns I've sung, the books I've read, the organizations which I support. While many of the theological voices in the Mennonite church have taught me to be "content to suffer" in the face of violence against women, I am encouraged by those voices which bring a message of liberation and hope. This is the message which I believe needs to be conveyed in practical ways to women who suffer from patriarchal violence.

For in the end, having written this paper, it is the voices of suffering women which linger in my mind: the voice of a woman telling me how prayer helped her to endure the beatings of an abusive husband; the voice of a woman minimizing the sexual abuse she experienced as a child saying, "It's not a big deal, I don't want to sound like I'm always complaining"; The voice of a woman who was raped asking, "Who can I tell in the church?"; the inner voice which has counselled me to accept and endure and minimize the violations which I have experienced. Voices such as these spur us onto further theological reflection, both re-examining past assumptions and articulating new directions for our theology.

NOTES

1. "Although the scholars who write systematic theology are generally silent on the topic, there remains a substratum of conviction among many Mennonites ... that suffering is salvific, purgative, and inevitable." *The Mennonite Encyclopedia*, s.v. "Family" p. 863.

2. *The Mennonite Hymnal* (Scottdale, Pa.: Herald Press, and Newton, Kans.: Faith and Life Press, 1969).

3. Mary Oyer, "Introduction," MH v.

4. The hymns found in the *Hymnal* are from a variety of Christian traditions. The compilers state their openness to hymns written within the Mennonite tradition, but they determined that hymns would not be included in the *Hymnal* simply because they had Mennonite origins. [Mary Oyer, *Exploring the Mennonite Hymnal* (Newton, Kansas: Faith and Life Press, 1980), 68.] Thus the theology found in the *Hymnal* is not uniquely Mennonite, except insofar ass the compilers who have edited this collection were Mennonite. The Mennonite or non-Mennonite nature of the theology found in the *Hymnal* is not an issue in this study, as the motive for examining the hymns is that they are indeed used in worship in contemporary churches and thus reflect and inform popular theological understandings.

5. "Bless, O My Soul, the Living God," MH 72.

6. "Sing Praise to God," MH 21.

7. "Hail to the Lord's Anointed," MH 113; see also "Sing Praise to God," p. 21.

8. "Be Still My Soul," MH 73.

9. "Jesus Thy Boundless Love to Me," MH 266.

10. "O Love Divine," MH 306.

11. "O Love Divine," MH 306.

12. "O For a Faith That Will Not Shrink," MH 259.

13. More Love to Thee, O Christ," MH 539.

14. He Leadeth Me, O Blessed Thought," MH 543.

15. "Be Still, My Soul," MH 73.

16. "How Beauteous Were the Marks," MH 103.

17. "Forty Days and Forty Nights," MH 144.

18. "How Shall I Follow Him," MH 349.

19. "Be Still, My Soul," MH 73.

20. Marcus Smucker, in his dissertation "Self-sacrifice and self-realization in Mennonite spirituality" (Union Graduate School, Cincinnati, Ohio, 1987, p. 63), provides an interesting discussion on the shift in Mennonite theology on views of suffering. Suffering for the Anabaptists entailed physical torture (for example, "Christ's servants follow Him to death, And give their body life and breath, On cross and rack and pyre." "He Who Would follow Christ," MH 344) Over time, however, Mennonites were influenced by the Pietists who understood suffering on a more

cerebral level. Regardless of the origins of this pietistic theology, its presence in the *Hymnal* (and its prevalence in comparison to Anabaptist hymns) is significant for the formation of popular theology in the Mennonite church.

    21. John Howard Yoder, *The Politics of Jesus* (Grand Rapids, Michigan: William B. Eerdmans Publishing Company, 1972).

    22. In Chapter 9 of *Politics* Yoder emphasizes that revolutionary subordination is possible for the Christian because they know that they are morally free. He writes, "It is because she knows that in Christ there is no male or female that the Christian wife can freely accept that subordination to her unbelieving husband which is her present lot." (p. 191) Yoder nowhere specifically states that contemporary women should be submissive to their husbands, yet in a book whose aim is to show the relevances of a New Testament ethic for contemporary readers, such an interpretation of his work is not far-fetched.

    23. Mennonite Central Committee Taskforce on Domestic Violence, "Introduction," in *The Purple Packet: Domestic Violence Resources for Pastoring Persons, Wife Abuse* (Winnipeg: Mennonite Central Committee Canada, 1987), 1.

    24. Mary Pellauer, for example, grew up in an abusive environment, while Marie Marshall Fortune and Joy Bussert have worked extensively in a pastoral role with battered women.

    25. Marie Marshall Fortune, *Sexual Violence: The Unmentionable Sin* (New York: The Pilgrim Press, 1983), xiii.

    26. Di Brandt, "Three Poems," *Prairie Fire*, 11 (1990), 183.

    27. For example, in an annotated bibliography of Mennonite writings on peace and nonresistance, violence against women is not seen as a peace issue. In their preface the editors admit that identifying precisely what is a peace issue was difficult, and they do cast a broader net than militarism, focussing also on justice issues such as race relations. The lack of any reference to incest, child abuse, or wife battering thus reflects the dearth of Mennonite writings on the subject. Willard M. Swartley and Cornelius J. Dyck, eds., *Annotated Bibliography of Mennonite Writings on War and Peace: 1930-80* (Scottdale, Pennsylvania: Herald Press, 1987).

    28. Fortune, *Sexual Violence*, p. 7.

    29. Yoder, *What Would You Do?* (Scottdale, Pennsylvania: Herald Press, 1983), 19.

    30. For an excellent discussion of patriarchy from a Canadian perspective see Lorraine Berzins, Phyllis Drennan-Searson, and Vern Redekop, eds. *Family Violence in a Patriarchal Culture* (Ottawa: The Church Council on Justice and Corrections and the Canadian Council on Social Development, 1988), 36-45.

    31. For example, women of color have an added burden of suffering as they face institutional racism when they do seek help from abuse. Joy M. K. Bussert, *Battered Women: From a Theology of Suffering to an Ethic of Empowerment* (New York: Division for Mission in North America, Lutheran Church in America, 1986), 37.

    32. Phyllis Trible, *Texts of Terror* (Philadelphia: Fortress Press, 1984).

    33. See, for example, "Litanies, Psalms and Songs," in *Sexual Assault and Abuse,* edited by Mary D. Pellauer, Barbara Chester, and Jane Boyajian (San Fran-

cisco: Harper and Row, Publishers, 1987), 225-247.

34. Bussert, *Battered Women*, 65-66.

35. Joanne Carlson Brown and Rebecca Parker, "For God So Loved the World?" in *Christianity, Patriarchy and Abuse*, ed. Joanne Carlson Brown and Carole R. Bohn, (New York: The Pilgrim Press, 1989), 3.

RESPONSE

Harriet Sider Bicksler

I'm not a theologian; I'm not a mental health professional; I'm an ordinary person who happens to be in church leadership at this particular point in our history as Mennonites and Brethren in Christ. Therefore, I have chosen to respond experientially, out of my experience of how theology has been worked out. As a lifelong member of the Brethren in Christ Church, I have been taught certain ways to behave based at least in part on theological understandings which were internalized by those before me and which I have also internalized. So I begin by adding the sources of my views about suffering to those Carol has listed; then I want to comment on the dissonance I feel between "suffering servant" peace theology and appropriate responses to abuse, to add a few comments about "perfectionism," and to raise several questions which I believe the theologians among us need to help us address.

SOURCES

1. *My mother.* Although I have tried very hard to distance myself from parts of my mother's personality that I have found troubling, I also know that she has been a powerful role model for me and that I am in many ways very much like her. Mother grew up in a strict, plain Brethren in Christ home, the oldest of six children. I never knew my grandfather, but I remember my grandmother as a stern but godly woman. In a few conversations I've had with my mother and my uncle about their childhood, I've put together a picture of a home where there were high standards of behavior, where faith was taken very seriously, and where few emotions (positive or negative) were displayed. I don't know that there was any abuse, although I have suspected (because of some evidence from my uncle and his family) that there may have been harsh physical punishment, and I am certain that approval was withheld when wrong was done or even when praise would have been appropriate. Consequently, she grew up easily susceptible to assaults on her self-esteem.

My mother, however, has always been a strong and intelligent woman. She was the only one in her family to graduate from college (with honors)--an achievement she accomplished on her own. I have often wondered what she might have done had she not married (at age 27 in 1939). My father's ambition was to be a foreign missionary, something he chose at least in part to overcome his own lack of self-esteem. It was a calling I don't believe my mother ever felt herself. But as a good, dutiful, submissive wife, she submerged her own desires (if she even knew what they were) and went with him first to northern Saskatchewan and then to southern Africa where I was born. I believe that my mother fully enjoyed her missionary life and has never regretted those years, but I don't think that she would have chosen that life.

The behaviors I saw in my mother and internalized from her include these:

1. Sacrifice yourself for your husband and children (expressed in never saying what you want or always taking the smallest piece, or going without something so that someone else can have). What you want is not nearly as important as what others want.
2. Resign yourself to the way things are. I've heard her say many times, "I just have to accept things"--even when it's obvious that everything in her doesn't want to accept things.
3. Submit to authority (of your husband, of the church, etc.)
4. Never express your anger openly. (Hold it in because as a "good Christian woman" you're not supposed to be angry). Allow your anger to spill out in more subtle passive-aggressive ways.
5. Be perfect. Although I know that my mother is not perfect, she always gives the impression of being a morally upright, godly woman who could not possibly have a bad thought in her head.
6. Feel guilty for not being perfect.
    (When I read the above list to my husband, he protested, "You didn't learn all that. *You* don't always sacrifice yourself for us; you don't submit to my authority!" He's right, but I still *feel* at some level like I should because that was the model I had. Intellectually, I don't believe all that, but I am continually amazed by how difficult it is to change behavioral patterns.)

2. *Hymns*: I too learned theology from hymns, although I'm not familiar with all of the ones to which Carol refers. In addition to glorifying suffering, there are hymns I sang as a child and adolescent which reinforce the themes of submission and lack of self-esteem which I learned in my family.

BENEATH THE CROSS OF JESUS:

Upon the cross of Jesus
Mine eyes at times can see
The very dying form of one
Who suffered there for me.
And from my smitten heart with tears
These wonders I confess
The wonder of his glorious love
And my own worthlessness...
Content to let the world go by
To know no gain nor loss
My sinful self my only shame
My glory all the cross.

I LAY MY SINS ON JESUS:
I lay my sins on Jesus,
The spotless Lamb of God...
I long to be like Jesus,
Meek, loving, lowly, mild.

I GAVE MY LIFE FOR THEE:
I suffered much for thee,
More than thy tongue can tell
Of bitterest agony,
To rescue thee from hell;
I've borne, I've borne it all for thee,
What hast thou borne for me?

3. *Pacifist and feminist theology:* I have read the same kind
of theology to which Carol refers. In my case, my pacifism predated
my feminism; that is, I grew up in a patriarchal peace church! My
point is that I internalized all the good peace theology about the
model of "the suffering servant" long before I became aware of how
certain interpretations of that model have been damaging to women.
Now it is difficult to put feminist critiques together with traditional
Anabaptist peace theology. Which is right? What are the best, most
biblical aspects of each?

DISSONANCE BETWEEN THE "SUFFERING SERVANT" MODEL AND APPROPRIATE RESPONSES TO ABUSE:

1. *Listen to the Bible, to these words about Jesus:* "He was oppressed and afflicted, yet he did not open his mouth; he was led like a lamb to the slaughter, and as a sheep before her shearers is silent, so he did not open his mouth" (Is. 53:7; notice the female pronoun for sheep!). Or, "Christ suffered for you, leaving you an example, that you should follow in his steps...When they hurled their insults at him, he did not retaliate; when he suffered, he made no threats" (1 Pet. 2:21,23). Immediately following this latter passage are instructions for wives to be submissive to their husbands--to win their husbands "without talk," to be gentle and quiet. These instructions are in turn followed by *brief* instructions to husbands (to respect the "weaker partner") and then by more about suffering: "If you should suffer for what is right, you are blessed" (1 Pet. 3:14). Is it any wonder that women have connected Christ-like suffering (accepting in silence whatever abuse is dished out) with submission to abuse by their husbands? If right is defined as submitting to husbands, isn't that suffering for what is right?

2. *As a pacifist, I believe in the suffering servant model*; in the context of the question of war, I resonate with the quotations Carol has used from *The Politics of Jesus* (and with Gayle Gerber Koontz's analysis of redemptive resistance). I am opposed to the death penalty, and I think that the prison system, by and large, does not facilitate restoration or reconciliation. When I heard the nation and the President breathing out murderous threats against Saddam Hussein or when I hear family members of a murder victim swear vengeance on the killer, I am troubled because such behavior feels profoundly unChristian. I especially find it difficult to sympathize with family members who--years after the murder--are still filled with hate and thoughts of revenge toward the perpetrator and who cheer when he/she is executed.

Yet more recently, as I've learned about abuse of women and reflected on my own dysfunctions, I have come to realize how difficult it is to apply, in a healthy way, the concept of the suffering servant to a woman's response to abuse. For women who have grown up in our churches, there are many things that come together to create a situation where abuse can happen. Not only is there the strong teaching about obedience and following Jesus, the suffering servant, but there is also a lot of talk about "absorbing violence". We're taught to forgive (70 x 7), we don't get angry, and we don't complain about our lot in life. Part of submission has also often been a process of devaluing ourselves--believing that we have done something wrong to deserve the abuse or that what we think is not important. To be the ideal Mennonite or Brethren in Christ woman is to be a self-sacrificing, self-effacing, submissive peacemaker, willing to suffer almost anything for righteousness' sake.

Meanwhile, Mennonite and Brethren in Christ women and children are being hurt and Christian men are responsible for their hurt. To continue to preach the efficacy of suffering servanthood without some moderating word to abused women is to be, I believe, at least partially responsible for their abuse.

THE ADDED DIMENSION OF PERFECTIONISM

The Anabaptist understanding of discipleship is demanding. It is costly; the standards are high. In the Brethren in Christ Church in which I grew up, the idea of costly discipleship was accentuated by the doctrine of sanctification--a second work of grace (following the new birth) in which "the body of sin is destroyed," the carnal mind is done away with, self is denied, the old man is put away. The end result of all this is that if we have an experience of sanctification, we feel like we have to be perfect. We can't fail; we can hardly even be human. This is true not only for women who can't resist evil when it's done to them, don't talk back, don't feel angry, and who must be unfailingly sweet and loving and forgiving, but also for men who have no healthy outlet for their emotions (especially "negative" ones like anger and frustration). Guilt is a constant companion as we're well aware that we're not measuring up to what we think is required.

ISSUES AND QUESTIONS

1. *Re-interpretation of submission and suffering:* Jesus chose to suffer. Unlike most abused women, he knew from the beginning what he was doing and why. There was an ultimate purpose in his suffering. (I'm not sure that this really answers the objections of some feminists who see the doctrine of the atonement as encouraging martyrdom and victimization--in their view, Jesus was the ultimate victim of child abuse at the hands of his father--but it is a beginning.) Christ was the "once and for all" sacrifice (Heb. 10:1-18). Some have said that he suffered so we don't have to (e.g., Marie Fortune, in "The Transformation of Suffering," *Christianity, Patriarchy and Abuse: A Feminist Critique*, 145).

How do these ideas fit with suffering violence at home? We need some help in understanding the difference between Christ's suffering and our own. Jesus suffered on the cross to atone for us, so that we don't have to atone for ourselves. Perhaps we have been taught the wrong things about the cross; perhaps it is even presumptuous to use Christ's cross (a one-time event in history) as a model for suffering.

2. *Standing up to unjust suffering*: Jesus himself did not always turn the other cheek (see John 18:19-24), and Paul invoked his Roman citizenship to avoid a flogging and to call his accusers to account for their actions (Acts 22:25). Is it possible to formulate a theology of suffering that does not do away with suffering servanthood as a model for dealing with violence, but which helps to empower women and others to encourage and expect justice and right behavior?

3. *Violence in war vs. family violence*: During the recent Persian Gulf War one of the questions I heard most frequently was, "What do you do with someone like Saddam Hussein?" The implication was that an evil person deserves to be punished, to have violence returned, etc. We peace people think we have answers to that question when it's at the international level (or even when it's a mugger or a rapist in a dark alley), but what about when the evil person is our spouse or our father or our pastor? Do we submit, suffer, avoid, retaliate, or something else? What are the parallels as well as the differences between violence in war and family violence?

4. *Making theology practical*: Implied in the last set of questions is the issue of bringing theology down to a practical level. It's one thing to theologize about how to deal with an enemy if it's another country because as Mennonites and Brethren in Christ conscientious objectors we can choose to avoid the issue by not going to war, but what if the enemy is at home and someone you simply can't avoid? What real help can we offer women who very much want to be peacemakers in the best sense of the word, but who need empowerment in their struggle against violence at home?

5. *What about men?* Carol's paper has almost exclusively addressed the issue of suffering from the point of view of women (why women are content to suffer and allow themselves to be victims of violence). But is there something about peace theology and our theology of suffering that makes men prone to violence? How are men able to espouse a theology of nonviolence in the world and then beat their wives and children and sexually abuse them at home?

One simple answer is "sin," but that doesn't satisfy me; I want to understand more. Do Mennonite and Brethren in Christ men feel so powerless in the world (emasculated in a sense because they don't participate in the manly rituals of war, etc.) that they need some place where they can exert their power? Are we like Charlie Brown who loves mankind, but can't stand people (we're good at

universalizing but not particularizing love)? Or have we simply con-
fined our peace teaching to the issue of war and failed to relate it to
our homes, churches and communities?

I don't believe we will succeed in stopping family violence if
we only empower women. Men also need a different sort of
empowerment which perhaps our peace theology has prevented.
For wholeness and health, I think we must work together.

The following statement was compiled from reports of listeners in each of the process groups at the consultation. It should be seen as a preliminary report and not as definitive in any way.

LISTENERS REPORT FROM THE CONSULTATION

I. HOW DOES WOMEN'S EXPERIENCE WITH VIOLENCE AND VIOLATION SHAPE OUR PEACE THEOLOGY?

1. We are forced to acknowledge the existence of abuse as a problem among us as a Mennonite people.

2. Mennonites (especially women) are not exempt nor protected from violence and violation because of our peace theology. When this violation occurs from leaders in the peace churches, our very peace theology lacks integrity.

3. Beginning with women's experience is a new way of doing peace theology. Credentials related to experience and life are as important as academic credentials for doing this work.

4. Women's experience with violence and violation questions traditional theological categories and assumptions concerning the meaning of suffering, submission, headship, the cross, obedience, forgiveness, servanthood and Christology.

5. Women's experience of violation questions the absolute value we have put on marriage and the family. It questions placing the permanence of marriage above the safety of self.

6. The experience of women suggests that peace theology may subtly undergird patriarchy. Since most peace theology has been articulated by men, women's experience of violence has not been adequately addressed.

7. Violence against women forces us to see violence issues systemically.

8. Women's experience challenges our theological and worship language.

II. HOW HAS PEACE THEOLOGY INFLUENCED OR
SHAPED WOMEN'S EXPERIENCE?

1. "Peace," "love of enemy," "nonresistance" have implied passivity and silence (politeness) in the face of abuse.

2. Suffering and powerlessness have been glorified or elevated
to virtues.

3. Patriarchal culture, on one hand, and a nonresistant peace
theology on the other, have been collapsed into a "passive
nonresistance" understanding for women.

4. A selective Christology, or "following a nonresistant Jesus"
has caused women to accept powerlessness as a normal,
desirable state.

5. Peace theology provides a way for us to raise violence
against women as a peace and justice issue.

6. "Redemptive resistance" pushes us towards creative solutions.

7. Peace theology has helped us to see that issues are not just
personal or ecclesial, but systemic.

8. Women's models within peace theology have not been
highlighted or celebrated as ways to resist violence.

9. Anabaptism has a history of "over-againstness" when it
comes to challenging the state, but never has challenged
patriarchy per se. Perhaps this is the time to do so.

III. WHERE DO WE GO FROM HERE?

1. Develop a church-wide grievance policy. Because patriarchy
protects perpetrators, we need new ways to systemically
address violence against women. Issues of financial
assistance, safety, congregational care, and leadership possibilities once rehabilitation has occurred for perpetrators,
should be addressed.

2. Provide more arenas for dialogue and theological formation. Especially important are places for academics/theologians and practitioners to dialogue.

3. The findings of this consultation should also be shared with those writing the new [Mennonite] confession of faith.

4. Sensitivity in use of language in theology and worship is critical.

5. The findings of this consultation should influence the teaching of Bible and theology at all of our Mennonite colleges and seminaries. (The lack of attendance of representatives from many of these institutions was noted.)

6. We need to focus on listening to the stories of survivors.

7. We need to develop dialogue among women who differ in their theological understandings and personal experiences.

8. We need to develop mechanisms for victims/survivors to help break the silence in our congregations and institutions.

9. The silence of men and their pain must also be broken.

BIBLIOGRAPHY

Andolsen, Barbara Hilkert; Gudorf, Christine E.; and Pellauer, Mary D., eds. *Women's Consciousness, Women's Conscience.* Minneapolis: Winston Press, 1985.

Anglican Church of Canada. Report to the General Synod 1986. *Violence Against Women: Abuse in Society and Proposals for Change.* Toronto: Anglican Book Centre, 1987.

Berzins, Lorraine; Drennan-Searson, Phyllis; and Redekop, Vern, eds. *Family Violence in a Patriarchal Culture.* Ottawa: The Church Council on Justice and Corrections and the Canadian Council on Social Development, 1988.

Brown, Joanne Carlson, and Bohn, Carole R., eds. *Christianity, Patriarchy and Abuse.* New York: The Pilgrim Press, 1989.

Bussert, Joy M. K. *Battered Women: From a Theology of Suffering to an Ethic of Empowerment.* New York: Division for Mission in North America, Lutheran Church in America, 1986.

Fortune, Marie Marshall. *Keeping the Faith.* San Francisco: Harper and Row, Publishers, 1987.

_____. *Sexual Violence: The Unmentionable Sin.* New York: The Pilgrim Press, 1983.

Frantz, Nadine Pence, ed. "Women: Bearing the Cross of Discipleship" *Women's Concerns Report* 89 (March-April 1990).

Golding, Gail. *Hands to End Violence Against Women: A Resource for Theological Education.* Toronto: Women's Inter-Church Council of Canada, 1988.

Koontz, Gayle Gerber. "Freedom, Discipleship and Theological Reflection." *Freedom and Discipleship*, 169-175. Ed. Daniel S. Schipani. Maryknoll: Orbis Books, 1989.

Martin, Steven P. "The Presence of Violence in the Mennonite Church and Family Systems." M.Th. thesis, Waterloo Lutheran Seminary, 1990.

Mennonite Central Committee Taskforce on Domestic Violence. *Broken Boundaries: Resources for Pastoring People, Child Sexual Abuse.* Mennonite Central Committee United States, 1989.

_____. *The Purple Packet: Domestic Violence Resources for Pastoring Persons, Wife Abuse.* Winnipeg: Mennonite Central Committee Canada, 1987.

Metzler, Ethel Y., ed. "Incest" *Women's Concerns Report*, 83 (March-April 1989).

Paetkau, Mabel, ed. "Focus on Family Violence" *Women's Concerns Report* 23, 24 (December 1978, January 1979).

Pellauer, Mary D.; Chester, Barbara; and Boyajian, Jane., eds. *Sexual Assault and Abuse: A Handbook for Clergy and Religious Professionals.* San Francisco: Harper and Row, Publishers, 1987.

Rempel, Melita, ed. "Wife Abuse" *Women's Concerns Report*, 74 (September-October 1987).

"Too Close to Home: Domestic and Sexual Violence." *Daughters of Sarah* 13:4 (July-August 1987).

To order any of these publications or to receive a complete listing of other IMS publications, please contact the Institute of Mennonite Studies, 3003 Benham Avenue, Elkhart, IN 46517-1999; 219/295-3726.